The Age of Annoyance: Managing our Frustrations with Information Overload

Gavin Jocius

www.annoyance.us

Cover Illustration Copyright © 2011 by Immanuel Kester
Cover & website design by Immanuel Kester
First Edition
Copyright © by Gavin Jocius. All rights reserved.
ISBN 978-1-105-11223-2
Subject to the exception immediately following, this book may not be reproduced, in whole or in part, including illustrations, in any form (beyond that copying permitted by Sections 107 and 108 of the U.S. Copyright Law and except by reviewers for the public press), without prior permission from the author.
Printed in the United States

Disclaimer: The email marketing messages described in this book pertain to permission-based marketing only. Any direct replies and feedback included were collected from different sources – friends and colleagues in the industry – that adhere to email marketing best practices. Although the author has made every effort to ensure that the information in this book is correct, the author and publisher do not assume and hereby disclaim any liability to any party for any loss, damage, or disruption caused by errors or omissions, whether such errors or omissions result from negligence, accident, or any other cause. Some names and identifying details have been changed to protect the privacy of individuals and organizations. The views expressed within this book are that of the author and do not reflect those of the companies the author has worked for or been affiliated with – past, present or future. Finally, this book is not a "how-to" guide or manual for electronic marketing; it is simply a collection of observations made by a person who works on the Internet; therefore, the opinions expressed in this book should simply be viewed as such.

For Lyra, whose entry into this world was my only deadline for getting this book finished. Without her, this would have simply been another of her Dad's unfinished projects, housed on one of the countless external hard drives scattered around the house.

Contents

Prologue	7
Introduction	9
E-mail vs. email?	17
Email is not dead	18
Operation spam Grandma	23
Viral Agents	30
Too many tweets might make a twat	31
Angry mob mentality, drive-by anonymity, and Soothsayer Schmidt	38
Flamebait & the rhetorical hammer of Godwin's Law	47
Information overload and the role of bloggers	60
Maintaining the appearance of control	74
We're all lazy until the machine stops	82
The Spazz	86
The age of annoyance – interruptions	88
The age of annoyance – speed & convenience	92
The age of annoyance – minor injustices	97

The age of annoyance – the new norm 102

Digital detox 106

OOO in the age of annoyance 110

Prologue (the Pope's email address)

Oh how the times have changed. In his 1999 book *Permission Marketing*, Seth Godin writes: "a Catholic bishop based in New York was even quoted as saying 'If Jesus were walking the earth today, I'm convinced He would have an e-mail address" (1999, 21). When Godin's book was written, the above statement must have seemed rather charming. Today, we know that Jesus, if he were walking the earth, would have multiple email addresses. Like President Obama, he would have one closely guarded address that he would only share with aides and trusted advisors. He would also have a general mailbox that an army of dedicated volunteers would manage. Like the Dalai Lama, who in 2011 had over two million followers, Jesus would also have a verified Twitter® account. He would also have an official Facebook® fan page, a dedicated YouTube™ Channel, Flickr™ and Foursquare accounts, an extremely high Klout score, and perhaps even a good old fashioned website where the About Page would include the site's communication credo: "Brothers, if you have a message of encouragement for the people, please speak" (Acts 13:15).

When I was working for an Email Service Provider (ESP) in Manhattan, the Vatican sent us, along with all other major ESPs, an email (or I guess it was more of a decree). The message included the newly appointed Pope Benedict XVI's email addresses (one in English and one in Italian) and instructions that we were to whitelist the Pope's addresses. Meaning, we were to make sure that both addresses were not included on any lists within our database – opt-in or otherwise. It was the Vatican's preemptive global unsubscribe campaign to make sure that the new Pope would not be bothered with an abundance of email. Annoying the Pope during his first week on the job seemed to be as deep a sin as one could commit in the digital realm. Needless to say, we obeyed the decree.

For me, receiving an email from the Vatican years ago symbolized the fact that everyone is communicating online and that Jesus and the Pope probably need email more than the rest of us because they have more followers than we do. They need to communicate, and email is a great way to do that – particularly to very large groups of people.

Today, we all have our own followers, but not all of our voices online are enlightened, informed or benevolent. We do not always send tweets of compassion or insight. We aren't regularly retweeting: "My dear brothers, take note of this: Everyone should be quick to listen, slow to speak and slow to become angry via @James1:19 #GoodAdvice." In fact, it is quite the opposite. We do not always think before we tweet; we have flame wars constantly online, and we inscribe our own personalized decrees to the world with ALL CAPS and angry emoticons. Why do we act this way?

As enriching as the Internet has become for many of us, it has also filled us with profound rage at times. While many of us are perfectly kind people in real life, there is just something about the Internet that makes us act a certain way. So if you have ever found yourself wanting to shout at your computer, perhaps send the Pope an angry email or tell someone on a discussion forum to "screw off," then I encourage you to read on.

Introduction (is "f*#& you!" an unsubscribe request?)

The 'liberating' effects of the Internet separate individuals from the common values and ethical norms they adhere to in the real world. - Elias Aboujaoude

Each morning, I start my day off by rolling out of bed and checking my iPhone™ on the way to the fridge/coffee pot. Before I do anything, I have to check my inbox where I am typically greeted by Groupon™ and LivingSocial® whose deals are then rushed off to the junk folder along with Facebook updates and the occasional notification of a new Twitter follower. This routine is very familiar to most people nowadays because our inboxes, John Freeman writes,

> have usurped the morning paper as a shaping context; many of us check it before we even glance at the news, let alone brew that first cup of coffee, making our email (and by extension ourselves) the most important information – for the shaping context – of the day (174).

Our inboxes provide us with that all important mental framework for what we can expect the rest of the day. It is our personalized link to the world that awaits us outside, and for whatever reason, something in the back of our minds keeps telling us that checking our emails should be the number one priority in the morning – more important even than nutrition.

I find that checking work email first thing in the morning is like playing Russian Roulette. As far as shaping the context of your day is concerned, you are essentially taking part in a dangerous game of chance. You hope you can just log-in, delete a few messages, respond to one or two, let people know you are up and moving, and proceed to having breakfast with a clear conscious – knowing that nothing major will happen in the next hour or so it takes to get ready and commute to work. But every once in a while: BAM!!! You scroll down to see an urgently marked message from your boss who is delivering news that could potentially ruin your morning. If we know that there is a good chance of bad news appearing in our inboxes, why do we bother? We could just learn to avoid our inboxes and enjoy a few moments of morning bliss, leaving the pain and misery for the office.

Unfortunately, most of us have no choice but to check our emails. We are constantly bombarded with such messages, resulting in "a frustrating marsh" that we have "no choice other than to tackle" (Paasonen, 165). We talk about getting "rid" of our emails, Sherry Turkle writes, "as though these notes are so much excess baggage" (11). Whether we like it or not, we relentlessly have to take out the electronic trash. In an independent market research survey, Microsoft® reports that 96% of survey respondents said that their email load either increased or stayed the same over the last year and that 37% said they spend half of their day reading or replying to email (Parr, 1). In a report published in 2009 by the University of California, San Diego, the average American consumes 34 gigabytes of content and up to 100,000 words cross our eyes in a single 24-hour period (Bilton). Most of us know that bad news potentially awaits us somewhere in those 100,000 words, and we are willing to take that risk in an effort to keep our inboxes from turning into unmanageable trash heaps. But the heap keeps growing. Unsubscribe.com reported that in 2010, 27 billion marketing emails were deployed, which amounts to roughly four emails per day for every person on the planet ... that is 7,300 emails annually for every person with an active email address (Wasserman, 1). With email marketing firms like ConstantContact® offering FREE 60-day trials and doing national ad campaigns, every company in the United States with a contact list (that has been properly obtained) has incentive to deploy email campaigns.

I would first like to mention that email marketers, at least all the ones I have dealt with, are not spammers nor are they Nigerian money launderers. They do not own porn servers in the Netherlands and most have not made millions of dollars pedaling penis enlargements. Email marketers do not send spam; they send *Bacn*. Bacn is the email you want, just not right now. While spam is unsolicited, the majority of all Internet users opt-in to receive some sort of Bacn. It is the monthly eNewsletters you receive from your alma mater or the deals you get from the travel website you used to book your last flight. Bacn is the stuff that clutters your already full inbox, even though at some point you thought you wanted it. Email marketers go to great lengths to make sure that you (and your email provider) don't send those messages into the junk folder. Still, there are a huge number of consumers who assume that email marketers are no different from spammers. In the words of computer scientist Gene Spafford, there are those who feel that if this were the ramp-up to the Black Plague in the Middle Ages, email marketers "would be trying to find ways to subsidize the purchase of pet rats" (Zittrain, 240). Consumers do not tend to like email marketers and if given the chance, they will make sure to let them know.

So if you find the trash heap that is your inbox bad, an email marketer's inbox is potentially much worse. If you start your day checking your email and find an angry note from your boss, an email marketer will find many more such messages. What follows is a sampling (typos and misspellings included) of what an email marketer's inbox may look like on any given morning:

> *Why do u keep on sending me the beepin e-mails.....lay off me....you donkeys or else*
>
> *GO AWAY*
>
> *For chrissake stop sending me your stupid e-mails.*
>
> *get off my computure you stop if you don't I will call the popo*
>
> *Stop sending me e-mails or i'll get my mum*
>
> *you can stop sending these– I'm giving up on you.*

fuck you, i'm a better editor than your biggest dickhead. go stuff it in your orifice

take me off your sucker list

you suke!!!1

oiiiii   no one likes you!!!!!!!!!!!!!!!!!!!!!!!!!! F****** of

STOP EMAILING ME PLEASE I DONT KNOW WHY I SIGNED UP FOR THIS

Please NO NOT SEND ME ANY MORE OF YOU RABISH

Please do not send me any more email advertising. I have a mind of my own and know what I want.

send to me the Pornography pictuer or photos

PLEASE STOP SENDING ME MESSAGES!!!!! JUST STOP! ANYWAY SHOPPING ONLINE IS LAMEEEE.......

I'd like to egg your company. You suck.

I like your dolphins not your Newsletter.

According to these random samples, email marketers must be doing something terrible, right? The fact is, most email marketers are just doing their jobs with full support of the law. CAN-SPAM is the federally enacted law that governs commercial email. Companies can receive fines of over $16,000 in the United States for every violation committed. As such, legitimate companies have great incentive to make sure that they are compliant. In 2006, CAN-SPAM was updated so that people sending commercial email cannot just slap a "noreply" address on a message. Unsubscribing now means someone can just hit the reply button or report a message as spam by hitting the abuse button in their email client, i.e., "This is spam." Abuse complaints can also be accompanied with an angry note or explanation as to why a user deems a message as "spam." Thus gave birth to the beloved "flaming unsubscribe." A popular email marketing service, MailChimp, reports that in 2010 they sent more than 40 million emails a day for "big giant corporations" (2010). The company states that "totally clean lists that are 100% double opt-in will get one or two abuse reports per 50,000 recipients" (2011). That means that on any given day, they could receive between 800 and 1,600 potentially angry replies.

Part of an email marketer's morning routine, therefore, may involve peering into an inbox where flaming unsubscribes and abuse complaints are collected, possibly read, and processed as quickly as possible. For an email marketing novice responsible for handling this job, it can be an incredibly depressing way to start the day. MailChimp reports that when people opt-in to receive email messages and then hit the abuse button "that usually means they don't remember you." MailChimp continues by stating that one should "make sure your "From:" and "Subject" contain your company name (so they'll instantly recognize you)" (2010). That may be the case, but I tend to think that people's reasoning for sending flaming unsubscribes are more primal and it really does not matter if they recognize your company or not. Voicing frustration is part of the not-so-subtle human condition. In a blog post entitled "I could just unsubscribe from your mailing list, but I'd rather be a jackass," journalist David Spark outlines two reasons why people respond to marketing emails with such anger. He writes:

> First, people will often project a past negative experience upon the next person. It's kind of like when a boyfriend or girlfriend projects their previous relationship's baggage on you. You just happen to be the next companion and your mate

didn't get the opportunity to vent on the last one. So you have to suffer now and take the bullet.

My second rationalization for this type of behavior is that some people are just a-holes.

Let me start with the latter point first. I disagree with Spark somewhat. We are *all* capable of acting like a-holes at one time or another. It is part of who we are as a species, and no one is above having a bad day and getting pissed off. Some of us just choose not to show our a-holes in public or to strangers. Spark's first point is spot on. I imagine someone just like me is waking up in the morning, making himself a coffee and minding his own business. Instead of waiting until he gets to work, he decides to risk it and check his work email. There it is – a frantic message from his boss stating that an important meeting is being rescheduled for earlier in the morning where he will be expected to give a presentation he has not prepared for. Then, an inbox alert notifies him that traffic is backed up on the highway. Then, eTrade tells him that his stocks are down. Then his kid's Principle sends him a message that he wishes to discuss little Billy's behavior in class. You get the drift. Unfortunately, somewhere in all that mess was a little email with a simple coupon for 25% off his next purchase at [insert random company here]. Whomever deployed that email message just happened to catch this person at the wrong time, and he certainly was not going to reply to his boss with a "Fuck you cocksucker." But his frustration had to be expressed somewhere because his day was already ruined, and that 25% off marketing message fit that need perfectly. Even if the user forgot that he signed up to receive email messages from said company or even if he no longer likes the company, why not just hit the unsubscribe button and be done with it? Well, he would rather be a jackass. Scientists from Keele University in the UK found that swearing can have a powerful painkilling effect, "especially for people who do not normally use expletives" (The Telegraph, 1). This is one reason, the researchers argue, why swearing is "an almost universal human linguistic phenomenon" and has persisted for centuries (The Telegraph, 1). For people who do not normally swear, yelling at what appears to be an anonymous email address may provide a nice emotional release from a morning already ruined by prior obligations and information overload.

The fact of the matter is that every email marketer I have either worked with or chatted with at conferences is a law abiding citizen. They take protecting user data very seriously and try to only send those messages you have asked for when you have asked for them. An email marketer's very existence depends on treating one's email address and identity with the greatest of care, following the laws and regulations set out for them. Email marketers do not call during dinner hours nor do they send you mountains of paper that end up in landfills. Email marketing messages are so easy to opt-out of, you don't even need to hit an unsubscribe button any more. You can just reply with "fuck off cocksucker" and the company sending the message is required to take you off their list (or at the very least mark your account as an unsubscribe). But despite all this, people still loathe marketing emails. Why? Why are we conditioned to despise the messages we asked for at one time? Why does it make us so angry to deal with something that takes less than a few seconds to fix?

The answer to these questions is simple – we live in the age of annoyance. Technology, electronic communications, gadgets, traffic, airline travel – as it all gets easier, it also seems to get exponentially more annoying. Annoyance is described as an unpleasant mental state that is characterized by such effects as irritation and distraction from one's conscious thinking. It can lead to emotions such as frustration and anger. Sound familiar? Many technology books have the word "annoyance" right in their titles. Just do an Amazon book search and you will find titles such as *Windows 7 Annoyances, PC Annoyances, Mac Annoyances, and Fixing PowerPoint Annoyances: How to Fix the Most Annoying Things about Your Favorite Presentation Program*. We love technology, but it also annoys the hell out of us. The best description of the era we now live in comes from the very popular YouTube clip of comedian Louis CK on the Conan O'Brian show. The clip is entitled "Everything is amazing [right now] and nobody's happy." I don't feel the need to describe the video here because (a) the title is self-explanatory, (b) chances are you have already seen the clip or forwarded it to a friend multiple times, (c) you either have a computer on somewhere next to you or a Smartphone on your person where you can go watch it now, and (d) me describing the video simply does not do it justice. It is hilarious and should be watched.

This book is written for marketers and communication professionals who now face a very difficult challenge of messaging people in an era of technology-induced hyper-annoyance. We continue to add new marketing channels to our already growing list, and with each new channel, we add both the ability to sell more, but we also increase our ability to annoy our customers. This book is also written for non-marketers, people who just want to make a bit of sense of the crazy world we now live in and perhaps better understand why we seem to lose control so easily when dealing with technology.

Is 'F*#& You!' an unsubscribe request? Yes it is. But more importantly, it is symbolic of the world that we now inhabit. It is a world where you would never say "fuck you, cocksucker" to the clerk at Whole Foods who offers you a savings coupon, but a world in which you would use the same phrase to respond to the faceless entity on the receiving end of an electronic message. How we manage our growing frustrations with information overload will determine whether this remains an age of annoyance or becomes a time of great creative growth. This book is a collection of ideas and observations that will hopefully help us move towards the latter and find ways that we can manage information without it completely frustrating us.

E-mail vs. email?

I want to address an important point before proceeding. On March 18, 2011, the AP Stylebook, also known as "the journalist's bible," announced that the hyphen used for the abbreviated version of "electronic mail" was being dropped (apstylebook.com). While I am not a journalist or newsman, I do plan on following the AP's recommendation for the simple fact that minimizing an extra keystroke in a book that mentions the word "email" countless times seems like a good idea. You can abbreviate "electronic mail" however you like. I am lazy; I choose email.

Email is not dead

[Email] is our electronic fidget. – John Freeman

> From: <postmaster@assp.local>
> To: Unknown recipient
> Subject: Spam report:
>
> *You reported spam.*
> *It now has been recorded.*
> *Thank you very very much.*
>
> – –
>
> *These words not asked for.*
> *Why are you in my email?*
> *Blue can, fat pink meat.*
>
> *bamboo flute on pond*
> *angry man shakes fists at sky*
> *e-mail clogged with spam*
>
> *www.spamhaiku.com*

At least once a quarter, I am forwarded a blog post stating that email is dead and/or is dying. *PC Mag* (Dvorak), *The Wall Street Journal* (Vascellaro) *Fox News* (Quain): there is no shortage of news outlets and magazines willing to forecast email's eventual demise. At conferences, seminars that seek to address this topic seem like support groups for anxious marketers worried about the long-term viability of their jobs. The fact is, email is not going anywhere. It is the cockroach of electronic communications – a persistent rascal that knows how to stay alive.

Arguing that email is dead becomes a moot point when a company like Groupon, aka "the fastest growing company ever," comes along and uses email as its primary means of communication (Steiner). Yes, Groupon's meteoric rise could also be met with an equally dramatic fall, but you have to give the company credit. Groupon's CEO, Andrew Mason, apparently chose email because "it's simple and universal" (Parr, 1). Like towels, bar soap or hammers, ease of use is what has given email its staying power. My personal belief, however, is that people expect email to die because it can be annoying, and humans have a tendency to either eradicate annoying things or work to make them less so.

In his book *The Tyranny of E-mail*, John Freeman writes that "e-mail has made us a workforce of reactors, racing to keep up with a treadmill pace that is bound for burnout and breakdown and profound anger" (5). Bloggers and best-selling authors Chris Brogan and Julien Smith joke at conferences by asking audience members "who here wants more e-mail? Raise your hands!" (197). And of course no one raises their hands. There is an expectation that one must reply to an email as quickly as possible. I am sure that you know of people in your office who send you an email and then follow it up with an IM: "did you get my email?" Sometimes, those people will even make a personal visit to your office/cubicle to make sure that you "saw" their email and, in a passive aggressive manner, hover over you until you open it. The question one has to ask is whether it is email itself or rather the people sending them that are truly annoying?

Email has gotten infinitely better than it used to be when I first created a hotmail account circa 1998. My GMail account now concentrates message content into easy to manage threads. My contacts auto-populate as I type them. GMail's IMAP tool allows me to access mail with MS Outlook Express. GMail automatically backs up copies of my emails as I type them, etc, etc, etc. Sure, I get this service for "free," knowing that intimate details about my finances, shopping preferences, and purchases are all sitting within climate controlled Google server farms around the world where algorithms tirelessly build an in-depth user profile on me. But I love the service and even find the targeted ads within my GMail account worth clicking on from time to time.

Despite the great, while at times creepy, work of the G-men, the annoying aspects of email always find their way into our inboxes. No matter how smart we make our spam filters, emails that we do not want will always sneak past and find ways to annoy us. Take these examples for instance. Below are samples of something you have undoubtedly seen in your inboxes over the last few years and have quite possibly caused some aggravation in your life:

>Sent from my iPad
>Sent from Blackberry on verison network
>Sent on the Sprint® Now Network from my BlackBerry®
>Sent via DROID on Verizon Wireless
>Sent from my iPod
>Sent from my MetroPCS Wireless Phone

>Sent on the Now Network from my Sprint® BlackBerry
>Sent from my BlackBerry® smartphone with SprintSpeed
>Sent from my HTC Touch Pro2 on the Now Network from Sprint®.
>Sent via BlackBerry by AT&T
>Sent from my Android phone with K-9 Mail. Please excuse my brevity.
>Sent from my BlackBerry® wireless device from U.S. Cellular
>Connected by MOTOBLUR™ on T-Mobile
>Sent via my BlackBerry from Vodacom - let your email find you!

>Sent on the TELUS Mobility network with BlackBerry
>Sent from Yahoo! Mail on Android
>Sent from my LG phone
>Sent from my Palm Pre
>Sent from my HTC on the Now Network from Sprint!
>Sent from my Samsung Transform™

> Sent via Telus My Email 2.0
> Sent from my BlackBerry® wireless handheld from Glo Mobile.

Mobile device taglines are everywhere now. And you have to give the marketers who came up with them a bit of credit because they have basically found a creative way to send unsolicited spam that circumnavigates your spam filter and is legal, as far as I can tell. Spam, as you know, is unwanted commercial emails sent in bulk. People who adopt such taglines are basically sending unsolicited advertisements to each and every one of their email contacts on a daily basis. In the case of Canada, a bi-lingual country, some phones even spam in multiple languages:

> Sent wirelessly from my BlackBerry device on the Bell network.
> Envoyé sans fil par mon terminal mobile BlackBerry sur le réseau de Bell.

Think of these taglines as micro-spamming for a 140 character generation. And the catch is, there is no way for the end-user to unsubscribe from them. Writer Mark Helprin sums his feelings towards such taglines when he writes:

> 'from my BlackBerry.' Excuse me? From your BlackBerry? I don't think the purpose of this declaration is to explain the brevity of your message, as you could probably type *War and Peace* with one thumb tied behind your BMW. I think its purpose is an ad from BlackBerry to let me know that you have a BlackBerry. May your BlackBerry rot in hell (186).

Do people honestly care that you are "on the Now Network from Sprint®" or "on the TELUS Mobility network"? I do not conclude a hand-written letter to my Grandmother (she's the only person I write letters to) with "I love you Grandma. See you at Christmas. P.S. this letter was brought to you by the US Postal Service™." So why is it seemingly okay to do the same thing for email? In a 2007 article for *Slate* Magazine, Paul Boutin writes, "an e-mail that says 'Sent from my iPhone' conjures an image of a doofus who wants you to know he has an iPhone." Yes, there are people who like to brag that they waited in line to get the newest Apple product and including a tagline that exhibits that fact will make said person appear cool for a few weeks. After which time, everyone else will also own said product and the early adopter (aka "adopster") will look like a doofus – until of course he upgrades again in 6 months, and thus the cycle continues.

For the most part, people are simply too lazy to hide their mobile taglines. The opportunity cost of time spent locating the settings tab and removing the message is higher than the alternative. We would simply rather spam our friends and family and have them deal with the advertisement then devote precious seconds to removing it. That is why I feel that the most annoying aspect of email is us. From a purely technological standpoint, email has become a work of wonder. Email is like a beautifully engineered German automobile: it is fast and efficient. But if you put a reckless jerk behind the wheel during rush hour, that automobile becomes something you want to give the middle finger.

Operation spam Grandma

Zyngeist. (noun) – Being on the cutting edge of the very latest VampireVille-Mafia-Scrabble Facebook games with which to relentlessly spam friends, family and random people you met once at a meeting. – Alex Blaggs in *FastCompany*

From a marketing standpoint, our mothers are ideal people to spam. I use the term "spam" here with a great deal of liberty to include any form of solicitation: phone calls, letters, emails, etc. Our moms love us; they listen to us; they trust us (we hope), and they are a proven market segment – having bought girl scout cookies and school fundraising items from us over the years. Recently, I happened upon the website momspam.net. The website states:

> YOU KNOW THOSE FORWARDS your mom fills your inbox with week after week, year after year? Well, this MOTHER'S DAY, you can return the favor by using Mom Spam. A site that features all the best FORWARDS we thought were just too good NOT to pass along.

The website is basically a large catalogue of cheesy pictures of dogs dressed up like superheroes, monkeys holding kittens, and spiritual misquotes that you can easily "pass on" to your mother or friends. It is the type of material many of the moms I know would get a kick out of and forward to us on a semi-regular basis. Well, momspam.net allows us to return the "favor." We open and read such ridiculous messages because of our trusted relationships with our mothers, and when we forward such "spam" to them in return, we can always expect them to do the same. Our mothers don't unsubscribe from our emails and almost always click-thru. That is why, from a marketing standpoint, they are ideal people for us to spam. They are the ultimate qualified lead. Unfortunately, on a one-to-one basis, they are a finite group, and as such, become a hard market to target en mass. But not for everyone.

For large corporations that are able to pool resources, it becomes easy to spam sizable groups of proud mothers. On April 4, 2011, Larry Page replaced Eric Schmidt as CEO of Google. In a major reorganization effort, Page allegedly sent a company-wide internal email that one reporter refers to as Page's "Spam Grandma for Cash" program (Elgan). While Google's PR department has yet to comment on the memo, subject-lined "2011 Bonus Multiplier," Page apparently stated that 25% of every employee's bonus is to be tied to Google's success in social media. Page wants employees to advocate Google's social networking features, the now launched Google+ project, to their family and friends. "When we release products, try them and encourage your family and friends to do the same," Page allegedly wrote in the memo (Elgan). Whether Page's memo is real or not, it is indicative of the affinity marketing efforts that are at the heart of social networks and why we can effectively spam our grandmothers/mothers/friends/family/colleagues.

We trust our family and friends. In return, we open their emails, "like" their shared links, and "follow" their recommendations. In the Executive Summary of *Subscribers, Fans and Followers* © 2010, email marketing firm ExactTarget ® reports that "90% of people trust the recommendations of their Facebook friends" (12). If Google contacted me directly, I may open their solicitation, but I would stand a much better chance of doing so if the same offering was recommended by a friend. The 2009 David Duchovny and Demi Moore film "The Joneses," an obvious reference to the idiom *keeping up with the Joneses*, exhibits this fact in a rather exaggerated way. The movie is described as "a social commentary on our consumerist society [where the Joneses are] not just living the American dream, they're selling it" (imdb.com). The film is about an upper class family of four who move into a new McMansion-style house where the neighbors become envious of the Jones' lifestyle and extravagances. The "family," however, is nothing more than a live-in corporate sales team designed to solicit mass consumption of beauty products, golf clubs, and skateboards through referrals and word of mouth. Debonair, stylish and cool, the Joneses are the most dangerous type of con-men because they are likable; they are people you feel you can trust.

While the concept of salespeople posing as a suburban family may seem a bit far-fetched, similar versions of such con jobs have been around for, one can assume, as long as there have been commercial markets or monetary investments. Affinity fraud, for instance, includes investment opportunities that solicit involvement by members of identifiable groups, particularly religious and ethnic communities. Such scams make use of the trust such groups have for each other. An obvious and very high-profile example of affinity fraud is that practiced by convicted felon Bernard Madoff, currently facing a 150 year prison sentence. Madoff is reported to have targeted "largely Jewish clientele across the eastern United States" (Leamer). Amongst Jewish communities, Laurence Leamer of the *New York Post* writes, "there was no one more revered and honored than Bernard Madoff" (Leamer). Madoff, who did make very large charitable donations to numerous organizations, managed to also get very high rates of return for his clients, most of whom did not question his means because of the apparent trust and admiration they had for him. Of course, it is not just the Jewish community that has fallen prey to such Ponzi schemes. Daren Palmer of Idaho is deemed to have created "a rural Western version of the kind of fraud Bernard L. Madoff operated in New York" (Yardley). Palmer is a "hometown investor" who promised an over 20% rate of return for his clients. Palmer recently pleaded guilty to federal criminal charges that he ran a $78 million Ponzi scheme. Mr. Palmer's deception, *New York Times* writer William Yardley writes "was remarkable for its scale, and its intimacy. His investors included his father, his brother-in-law, his neighbors, a car dealer, a builder whose son he coached in football, and others" (Yardley). Many of his investors were also members of Palmer's local Church of Jesus Christ of Latter-day Saints.

Cases like Palmer and Madoff are extremely unfortunate. Such Ponzi schemes have destroyed many people's savings, retirements and lives. In their book *Trust Agents,* Chris Brogan and Julien Smith argue that such examples force us to question what trust means in today's society, stating that:

> We are living in an age where the economic collapse of 2008 and 2009 shook our trust in our entire financial systems, compromised the viability of our retirement funds, and sent massive waves of distrust through London, New York, and beyond (8).

The authors argue that we are now facing a "trust deficit" where, "as a society, we no longer have confidence in advertising" (14). I have to disagree with Brogan and Smith somewhat on this point because, whether fully aware of it or not, people have <u>always</u> had reasons to be suspicious of advertisers. In his book, *Fables of Abundance: A Cultural History of Advertising in America,* Jackson Lears traces the less than favorable origins of the American Ad-man, writing:

> The first advertising agents were perfectly at home in the fluid, informal market settings favored by peddlers and assorted other confidence men. The skilled advertising agents could deftly manipulate the appearance necessary for success in the financial service trades that flourished amid the uncertainty of nineteenth-century business relationships (91).

American advertising was born out of deception. Selling elixirs, Indian herbs and all types of Oriental splendor, peddlers were some of this country's earliest capitalists. At times mistaken as pilgrims, early peddlers' intentions were "anything but pious" (67). Such "confidence men" gave the promise that "people could be released from all fear and anxiety if they would simply trust the technical expertise of the vendor" (99). Confidence, Lears argues, is another name for *hubris*, i.e., "to have confidence is to believe that the experts know best" (101). So while our recent financial crisis may have shaken our confidence in marketing and advertising, Ad-men have always tried to gain our trust and sell us things we do not necessarily need, and it is something we have had to deal with for centuries. I do, however, agree with Brogan and Smith in that we now live in an era of greater transparency. Illiterate settlers in the 1800s did not have Google on their PCs to check the ratings and reviews on Angie's list of travelling snake-oil salesmen posing as patent medicine men. They basically had to take what such men sold at face value, and hope that a firm handshake was the sign of an honest man. So while there may in fact be a trust deficit nowadays, there are also plenty of tools for us to validate someone's credentials.

Within our transparent online ecosystem, Brogan and Smith argue that there is a new brand of "pioneers" known as *Trust Agents* – non-sales-orientated, non-high-pressure marketers who use "the Web to be genuine and to humanize their business" (14-15). Trust Agents "use today's Web tools to spread their influence faster, wider, and deeper than a typical company's PR or marketing department might be capable of achieving, and with more genuine interest in people, too" (15). In short, Trust Agents are those folks who are heavily involved in social media, have lots of Twitter followers, write informative blogs, speak at conferences, etc. People like Cory Doctorow, Glenn Greenwald, and Mashable's Pete Cashmore come to mind when referring to Trust Agents. We have confidence in their opinions, for we see them as experts. Such people have a great deal of clout, and as such, people believe what they say. Unfortunately, when it comes to the galaxy of Internet users, the Cory Doctorow's of the world represent a tiny minority. Sure, there are companies like Klout.com that are working to provide tools where regular mortals such as myself can track the impact of our opinions, but the total number of real Trust Agents, I would say, is pretty miniscule in the grand scheme of things.

I do like the idea of Trust Agents. I think that it is important to humanize the web as much as possible and to allow people to build influence and distribute their knowledge without overtly trying to sell or market goods and services. But there is still a much larger issue with trust in general on the Internet – namely, there is simply too much of it. How do we know that Trust Agents are not selling themselves, their ideas, their own personal brands, their blogs, their books, their conferences, etc? On April 17, 2011, CBS *60 Minutes* did an investigative report on Greg Mortenson, co-author of *The New York Times* bestselling book *Three Cups of Team: One Man's Mission to Promote Peace ... One School at a Time*. Mortenson is also the co-founder of the Central Asia Institute (CAI), which is a non-profit that builds schools and provides education for needy children in Pakistan and Afghanistan. *60 Minutes* claims that many of the stories reported within the book did not take place, that most of the schools that the CAI claims to have built were not, and that the amount of funds CAI spends on promoting Mortenson's books and paying for speaking engagements exceeds that of comparable charitable organizations. The transcript of the program states:

> His point is that when Greg Mortenson travels all over the country at the charity's expense, he is promoting and selling his books and collecting speaking fees that the charity does not appear to be sharing in. According to the financial statement, the charity receives no income from the bestsellers, and little if any income from Mortenson's paid speaking engagements, while listing $1.7 million in "book-related expenses."
>
> Kroft: The $1.7 million that they spent for book-related expenses is more than they spent on all of their schools in Pakistan last year. (http://www.cbsnews.com/stories/2011/04/15/60minutes/main20054397.shtml)

I would argue that Mortenson, despite his apparent good intentions and service to humanity, may have fallen victim to his own hubris. He had a great deal of influence, more so than most company's PR departments, and he clearly had a genuine interest in people. But apparently, he was also an overconfident expert whose clout may have gotten the best of him, and thus became a living example of the proverb "pride goes before the fall." Like confidence men of the 1800s, there may be some Trust Agents whose intentions are not as pious as they make them out to be.

Despite the fact that we have a wealth of investigative information at our fingertips, even today we believe such online experts. But unlike our mothers and close friends, these are not always people we can trust. This is something we need to continue to be mindful of when operating online.

Viral Agents

No matter how smart we get, there is always this deep irrational part that makes us potential hosts for self-replicating information. - Neal Stephenson

It was not that long ago that people had to be convinced that it is okay to use the term "viral" for anything other than viruses. Today, attributing the term viral to phenomena that only vaguely remind us of viruses "has become common practice," according to Roberta Buiani (82). Computer viruses, viral videos, viral marketing, the term has become an accepted part of online culture. But in a 1996 article in *Fast Company*, Jeffrey Rayport had to reassure us, stating that "it's time to stop shying away from the ominous sound of it and embrace the enemy: viral marketing or v-marketing, if the term is too harsh" (1). Have you ever heard someone use the term "v-marketing"? No one finds the term viral marketing "too harsh" (at least that I know of). Ted, a respected online video site, has a credo that embraces the viral – "ideas worth spreading." Sure not all ideas are worth spreading, but good or bad, we spread them anyway. Our acceptance in applying the term viral to online phenomenon results in, Buiani writes, "not only a new way of understanding the notion(s) associated with the viral and the original agents (viruses) from which they emanate, but also a new way of reinterpreting the role of the user as active player" (83). We are viral agents – some of us more trustworthy than others. We are responsible for spreading massive volumes of content instantaneously over vast areas of digital space, and viruses make up part of our every day online existence. Whether fully aware of it or not, we do not see any issue with distributing media viruses. In fact, we take great pride in doing so. We just don't call it spreading viruses; now we call it sharing.

Too many tweets might make a twat

Some of my colleagues think a million, or perhaps a billion, fragmentary insults will eventually yield wisdom that surpasses that of any well-thought-out essay, so long as sophisticated secret statistical algorithms recombine the fragments. I disagree. A trope from the early days of computer science comes to mind: garbage in, garbage out. - Jaron Lanier

Two months before he was to become British Prime Minister, conservative leader David Cameron went on The Christian O'Connell Breakfast Radio Show. When asked about Twitter, Cameron replied, "I'm not on Twitter ... politicians you have to think about what we say and the trouble with Twitter, the instantness of it is ... too many tweets might make a twat" (Absolute Radio). Ironically, that last phrase was exactly the kind of sound bite that would have generated a great number of retweets. It is short, slightly vulgar and something that most people on Twitter can relate to; i.e., the ever presence of twats – unknowing fools who sends too many annoying tweets.

If you want to see an excellent satirical take on the annoying Twitter Twat, check out the online campaign "Re:cycled Tweet" by North Carolina-based advertising agency McKinney. As part of the campaign, viewers can watch a video of Brandon, "who sucks." Brandon enjoys angering others, has creepy pets, and tweets boring updates, e.g., "I hate Mondays." The video then introduces Reed, "who's awesome!" Reed enjoys chivalry, teaching children to read and frenchin' chicks (camera pans to Reed kissing a co-worker next to the copy machine). Reed, the video points out, hates only one thing: boring tweets. Since Reed is awesome, he decides to recycle Brandon's pathetic tweets to help charity. Reed adds Brandon's twitter handle, pastes in the boring tweet and adds the hashtag #recyclethis. In doing so, McKinney donates a penny for each recycled tweet to TRASHed, a recycling education program. Thus, Reed has "made Cyberspace a better place ... and Brandon sucks a little bit less."

One place you are likely to run across a Brandon is at conferences. They love to deploy boring and annoying tweets while in the company of their peers. Twitter, Behan et al point out, allows attendees to avoid some of the participation challenges that were once part of large lectures. Before Twitter, large lectures faced a few major participation problems, including:

> • Feedback Lag: There is lack of peer feedback in and by the audience
> • Student Apprehension: This factor stresses the fear of individuals in asking questions
> • Single Speaker Paradigm: Only-one-speaker syndrome leads to participation decrease (3)

Every tech conference I went to in the last year (South by SouthWest, Internet Summit, Bronto Summit, Book Expo America) all had official conference hashtags. According to Mashable, the 2011 #SXSW hashtag saw over 315,000 tweets, beating #BlackFriday by over 185,000 tweets. Twitter adds value to conferences, Behan et al state, because it "helps you reach out to others with similar interests, provides networking potential, and allows people who could not attend to gain some value from your experience" (7). Personally, I think greater research needs to go into qualifying that last statement about people who could not attend the conference and the value they gain by your tweets. For small educational conferences where you may get a couple hundred tweets, that is perhaps the case. But for large conferences like SXSW that produce hundreds of thousands of tweets, you run the risk of annoying your contacts with boring tweets and leading to what is known as "Twitter envy."

I will be the first to admit that I am both guilty of dishing out and receiving Twitter envy. In a *New York Times* article entitled "On Twitter, 'What a Party!' Brings an Envious 'Enough, Already!'" Amy Harmon describes Twitter envy as "tweets from attendees at elite conferences like TED and the World Economic Forum in Davos, Switzerland, [that] have prompted bitter ripostes, accusing the authors of showing off rather than sharing" (1).

Being at a large well-respected conference grants one the opportunity to show off to one's peers, i.e., act like a Brandon. It is the equivalent of being at a cool High School party and texting your friends to let them know you got invited while they didn't – and that there is beer at the party, plenty of cute girls (and/ or boys), a hot tub, good music, free food, a ping-pong table with beer pong, jell-o shots, a stripper pole in the basement, a hidden rock grotto, live bands, a DJ, bowling alley and tennis court – you get my point. Respected blogger Jeffrey Zeldman (@zeldman) tweeted March 1, 2011 that "People tweeting from #TED aren't sharing knowledge. They're letting you know they're at TED and reminding you you're not" (Scanlon, 1). I didn't even follow @zeldman at the time and I remember seeing his comment retweeted and getting a good laugh. @zeldman's post seemed to have struck a chord. I related to @zeldman's tweet because I wanted to be invited to TED2011 (a conference in Long Beach, California of the world's leading thinkers and doers), but I wasn't. In fact, I was part of a team that submitted numerous videos to TED's "Ads Worth Spreading" contest, the winners of which got a free trip and entry into the conference. Needless to say, our grassroots low budget entries, unlike the super bowl ads of Chrysler® and Volkswagen™, were not deemed "worth spreading" and were not selected. As such, my Twitter envy and rejection from the conference forced me to simply ignore Twitter until after TED was over. Sad, I know.

Instantaneousness is what makes Twitter both addictive and annoying, as real-time updates are a great way for us to remain informed, but it also makes us feel left behind when we are not constantly checking our feed. On Twitter's #numbers blog, it reports that there were "456 tweets per second (TPS) when Michael Jackson died on June 25, 2009 (a record at that time)" (blog.twitter.com/2011/03/numbers.html). In August of 2011, Twitter even launched an online commercial stating that it is "faster than earthquakes" making reference to the fact that it took 30 seconds for the August 23, 2011 earthquake to travel from Washington DC to New Work while tweets of the event spread almost instantly. Twitter allows us to receive information faster than Mother Nature. However, with speed comes a lack of careful thought and fact checking, items you would normally get when receiving news from traditional news outlets. Brooklyn-based designer Joe Newton (@TheJoeNewton) created a letterpress poster (that has since sold out online) that states "Google before you Tweet is the new think before you speak," which you can find on his site http://josephnewton.com/type. People need to stop and consider what they are saying sometimes before tweeting.

As a Canadian, I could not help but include the following example of how ill-timed tweets may go wrong. A 73-year-old Canadian election law, as *Vancouver Sun* reporter Gillian Shaw points out, "is proving to be a thorn in the side of a modern digital world" (1). Tweeters in Canada could face fines of up to $25,000 if a complaint is filed against them for misrepresenting election results. Section 329 of the Canada Elections Act states: "No person shall transmit the result or purported result of the vote in an electoral district to the public in another electoral district before the close of all of the polling stations in that other electoral district" (Shaw, 1). In the Twitterverse, tweeting the final score of a game or the winner of American Idol before someone has had the chance to watch either event is certainly annoying, but not illegal. I suppose the Elections Canada Commissioner simple wants users to practice restraint and allow the news media to first publish the official results. As far as Canadian elections are concerned, one is encouraged to Google before tweeting.

It should be noted that ill-timed tweets and online comments also take place in the United States. In the April 2011 murder trial NC v Brad Cooper, a judge banned all electronic devices, including cell phones and laptops, from the courtroom after comments about the trial appeared on WRAL.com, a local news website, from courtroom attendees. In United States v. Shelnutt (M.D. Ga. Nov. 2, 2009), a reporter for the *Columbus Ledger-Enquirer* was denied his request to use his cell phone to tweet to the newspaper's Twitter page. The Georgia federal court ruled that Rule 53 of the Federal Rules of Criminal Procedure prohibits 'tweeting' from the courtroom and that Rule 53 does not unconstitutionally restrict freedom of the press (Carton, 1). Rule 53 states that the "court must not permit the taking of photographs in the courtroom during judicial proceedings or the broadcasting of judicial proceedings from the courtroom" (Carton, 1). The court, according to Adriana Cervantes, looked at the definition of the word broadcasting in Webster's Third New International Dictionary and concluded that "the definition of broadcast includes casting or scattering in all directions and the act of making widely known" (10). As such, according to the Shellnutt court, "broadcasting" includes electronic messages (tweets) sent from the courtroom that "contemporaneously describe the trial proceedings and are instantaneously available for public viewing" (Carton, 1).

Despite these examples, tweeting in the courtroom, particularly in the United States, remains a contested issue. As of summer 2011, when this book was written, the US Supreme court had yet to consider whether Twitter should be allowed in court proceedings. As reported in *Time* magazine, "the Supreme Court has long held that the First Amendment generally requires trials to be open to the public – an openness principle that the court has, of course, declined to apply to its own proceedings" (Cohen, 1). As with the two cases noted above, however, rules regulating broadcasting in the courtroom vary state by state.

In May of 2011, the world got to witness what had the potential to be the world's most ill-timed tweets. Tweeting from Abbottabad Pakistan, IT consultant Sohaib Athar (@ReallyVirtual) has become known as the man who "unwittingly live-tweeted the events leading up to terrorist Osama Bin Laden's death" (*The Independent*). During what turned out to be the United States successful raid on the OBL compound, @ReallyVirtual tweeted: "Helicopter hovering above Abbottabad at 1AM (is a rare event)" and "The abbottabad helicopter/UFO was shot down near the Bilal Town area, and there's report of a flash. People saying it could be a drone" (*The Independent*). It wasn't until a week later when President Obama was interviewed by Steve Kroft on CBS's *60 Minutes* that the world got a sense of how top-secret this mission actually was. As the President said:

> You know one of the great successes of this operation was that we were able to keep this thing secret. And it's a testimony to how seriously everybody took this operation and the understanding that any leak could end up not only compromising the mission, but killing some of the guys that we were sending in there.
>
> And so very few people in the White House knew. The vast majority of my most senior aides did not know that we were doing this. And you know, there were times where you wanted to go around and talk this through with some more folks. And that just wasn't an option.

It has been reported that OBL did not have Internet access in his compound, but could you imagine if @ReallyVirtual's tweets or some similar online chatter were observed by one of OBL's curriers or trusted aides? What if @ReallyVirtual's tweets actually tipped off OBL, allowing him just enough time to escape before those choppers landed?

While it is certainly unlikely that such tweets would have changed the outcome, it does raise a lot of questions about communication in today's world. Basically, no matter where you go, someone is watching you. Even the world's most wanted man and the White House's most top-secret missions are not immune from the prying eyes of each and every one of us. Collectively, we are Big Brother 2.0, keeping a vigilant eye on the comings and goings of both the mundane and the all important. But with such power normally comes great responsibility. Could @ReallyVirtual have been held responsible for his actions had he tipped off OBL? I don't know, but it appears that Governments like Canada's are starting to address such issues – at least as they pertain to tweeting during federal elections. For now, @ReallyVirtual has been granted exponentially more Twitter followers and some Internet-notoriety, but had it gone another way, he would have been the very definition of how too many tweets might make a twat.

Angry mob mentality, drive-by anonymity, and Soothsayer Schmidt

Angry mob mentality's no longer the exception, it's the rule. –
NOFX

I love Canada. It is my home and native land. It is a beautiful country with great people. Canoe trips, Tim Horton's, poutine, and Crown Royal are all part of my DNA. Like all Canadians, I am extremely proud of what my country stands for and love to share Canada's commitment to multi-culturalism and peace-keeping around the world. Growing up watching the CBC, a company that aims to "bring diverse regional and cultural perspectives into the daily lives of Canadians," I felt that Canada could do no wrong, that Canadian shit don't stink (and in fact smells of roses like the kind Pierre Trudeau used to wear), and that we are pretty much the greatest country on Earth (cbc.radio-canada.ca/about/).

My naive view of Canada came to an abrupt end while attaining my undergraduate degree at the University of Toronto when one of my professors assigned the book *None Is Too Many: Canada and the Jews of Europe 1933-1948* to the reading list of one of our classes. In the book, the authors argue that during the Second World War, Canada's immigration policy, particularly as it pertained to Jewish refugees, was some of "the most stringent to be found anywhere in the whole world" (Abella & Troper, 35). Frederick Charles Blair, who was head of Canadian immigration under the Mackenzie King government, made a point of restricting access for Jews into Canada. During the Second World War, Blair admitted that he was convinced that the destruction of European Jewry was imminent and in a letter to a pro-refugee Anglican clergyman, Canon W.W. Judd, Blair stated that "he feared that Jews were facing virtual 'extinction' in Europe, but to allow more of them into Canada, he informed Judd, would not solve the problem" (Abella & Troper, 35). Canada basically closed its doors to Jewish refugees – a fact expressed in the title of the book, which refers to an anonymous senior Canadian official who, when asked how many Jews would be allowed entry into Canada after the war, said "none is too many."

There are parts of our heritage, like racist immigration policy, that many Canadians do not know about. Canadians like to keep our reputation as a peaceful and loving people intact, so there may be some of us who simply choose not to acknowledge the past. Perhaps it is the result of growing up watching the CBC, but anytime Canada does not live up to its well-polished image, it can come as a bit of a shock to us and even to non-Canadians. A modern-day example of this can be seen in the response to the riots that followed game seven of the 2011 Stanley Cup finals where the Vancouver Canucks lost to the Boston Bruins at home 4-0. Large crowds of hockey fans gathered in the streets of Vancouver to watch the game on outdoor monitors. After the game, riots quickly ensued; police cars were set ablaze; shops were looted; glass was broken and arrests were made. It was all very unfortunate and the world-wide media picked up on it, including NMAWorldEdition, the Taiwanese CGI animated studio made famous in the United States and abroad for its silly reenactments of major news events. The text for the Vancouver riot reenactment is as follows:

> Anarchy in the B.C. as Canuck fans riot. Canadians are known for being polite while Vancouver is famous for being a beautiful city. But there is a dark side – hockey. Hockey has long been a way for Canadians to release their pent-up anger. (Insert a shot of Canadians wearing modern-day clothing pushing a Mounty off a horse – Montreal circa 1955). Some packed gas masks to the Stanley Cup finals between the Canucks and the Boston Bruins. And when the Canucks lost 4-0 some fans began a 4-hour orgy of rioting and looting ... As the fans ran amok, they paused to pose for photos and to perform stunts. The next day, Canadians were out on the streets again cleaning up the mess. Peace and

order prevails again in Canada … until the next hockey game (youtube.com/watch?&v=8LBxFmixh70).

NMAWorldEdition's reenactment highlights some of the positive stereotypes of Canadians while sensationalizing our misanthropic "dark side" – triggered of course by hockey. As ridiculous as the reenactment is, I think they were wise for pointing out the fact that many rioters "paused to pose for photos and to perform stunts." While the riots in general make no sense to me, particularly when people in Egypt and Syria were, at the same time, risking their lives to riot for worthwhile causes, it seems absolutely outrageous to burn and destroy public property in our modern digital age where hundreds of revelers are recording all actions from multiple angles – all of which eventually can be uploaded to YouTube for public record and referenced by news agencies and prosecution lawyers.

So why did the Canucks riot? And more importantly, why did they do it in front of hundreds of cameras? Unfortunately, I cannot answer either of those questions with any level of certainty. I was not there and cannot draw any conclusions based simply on what was shown on TV and YouTube. If I had to guess at the first question, I would argue that the combination of booze, mild weather, and over-crowded streets gave rise to a powder keg that officials could not keep from blowing up. As for why people would commit crimes on camera, I have a theory and it involves the Internet.

As a society, we have grown accustomed to exhibiting terrible behavior online. Elias Aboujaoude is a psychiatrist at the Stanford University School of Medicine where he is the Director of the Obsessive Compulsive Disorder Clinic and the Impulse Control Disorders Clinic. Aboujaoude helped lead the largest U.S. study on problematic Internet use published to date. The study looked at the Internet habits of over 2,500 U.S. adults and revealed an "alarming rate of online pathological behavior that cut across geographic, socioeconomic, age and gender differences" (Aboujaoude, 10). Such behavior, the author noted, included "exaggerated sense of our abilities, a superior attitude towards others, a new moral code that we adopt online, a proneness to impulsive behavior, and a tendency to regress to childlike states when faced with an open browser" (Aboujaoude, 11). Anger tends to happen naturally for many people online. We are not taught to ridicule others on discussion forums, it just happens. Gentleness, common courtesy, and the little niceties that announce us as well-mannered, civilized, and sociable members of the species, Aboujaoude points out, "are quickly stripped away to reveal a completely naked, often unpleasant human being" (96). Most of us who have ever made a post on an online discussion forum have at one time or another experienced such behavior or have taken part in it. We may have said something in such forums that we would never have said in real life. The Internet simply allows us to flirt with our darker sides with very little consequence.

The best term that I have found for this type of irresponsible online behavior comes from Internet visionary Jaron Lanier. He refers to it as "drive-by anonymity" (63). As a web developer, I agree with Lanier's argument that design underlines ethics in the Digital World. Lanier argues that it is the design of the Internet that has given rise to trolling, flame wars, and "lutz" – the gratification of witnessing others suffer online (62). While there are social and economic factors that force some to be mean to others online, the ability to post anonymously online with very little recourse remains the most important factor for enabling trolling behavior. As Lanier writes, it "is effortless, consequence-free, transient anonymity in the service of a goal, such as promoting a point of view, that stands entirely apart from one's identity or personality" (63). As such, the very structure of the Internet, according to Lanier, is responsible for much of our pathological behavior online.

Ironically, cameras, video footage, internet cookies, IP geolocation, mobile device tracking locators, and other potentially incriminating devices are unable to stop people from acting stupid online. Take Anthony Weiner for instance, the New York Congressman who resigned from office on June 21, 2011 for getting caught tweeting lewd photos and "sexting" – most of which were easily accessible to the public online. As a high-profile politician, I think most people asked "what the hell was he thinking?" But this still did not stop him from doing something he probably never would have done without the apparent anonymity of the Internet. In August of 2009, nineteen year old Jonathan Parker broke into a house and stole two diamond rings. Once inside the house, he stopped to check his Facebook profile on the victim's computer, but never logged out (Marshall, 1). Needless to say, the police had plenty of information to locate the criminal via his FB account. Also in the summer of 2009, the wife of Sir John Sawers, the newly appointed head of the British Secret Intelligence Service M16, posted pictures of her husband, family and friends that detailed where they lived, took their holidays and where their children went to school. The posted data amounted to an extraordinary lapse in judgment, not to mention a serious security risk as the information could have potentially been used by hostile foreign powers or terrorists. As Liberal Democrat Foreign Affairs spokesman, Edward Davy writes, "normally I would welcome greater openness in government for officials or politicians, but this type of exposure verges on the reckless" (Hemming & Fincer, 2009). Whether you're a high profile politician or a juvenile criminal, everyone seems to act stupid on the Internet.

The above examples help highlight what Don Tapscott and Anthony Williams refer to as an "interactive ethos" (36). We have quickly learned to share all aspects of our lives with the people around us, without necessarily taking into account the security repercussions for both now and in the future. Former Google CEO, Eric Schmidt, famously stated that "I don't believe society understands what happens when everything is available, knowable and recorded by everyone all the time" (Jenkins). As reported in the *Wall Street Journal*, Schmidt predicted, apparently seriously, that "every young person one day will be entitled automatically to change his or her name on reaching adulthood in order to disown youthful hijacks stored on their friends' social media sites" (Jenkins). Being forced to change one's name may be a bit extreme, but many young kids will have some aspects of their early lives available on search results that they will most certainly regret when it comes time to look for a real job later in life.

So if we tend to act irresponsible online despite our actions being recorded and logged on servers, who is to say we would not do the same thing in real life? My argument is that the Vancouver riots mirrored the type of seemingly consequence free and fluid anonymity found on the Internet. In such an environment, normally polite and well-mannered people felt free to act irresponsible and, at times, cruel to other members of the faceless masses. This argument was expressed in an Editorial within one of Canada's national newspapers, *The Globe and Mail*:

> It was as if the supposed anonymity of the Internet had been transferred to the crowds of thousands, who felt invisible, all-powerful and therefore beyond punishment. (Some clung to this belief in invisibility even while giving interviews on camera to CBC-TV or the Vancouver Sun.) And now the Internet and other modern technologies, including the ubiquitous cell phone camera, are exploding that anonymity, and bringing the rioters out into the harsh light where they can be held responsible (2011).

The presence of cameras and video did not matter as many of the rioters did not stop to contemplate the long-term repercussions of their actions. Most rioters were basically practicing "drive-by anonymity" in the face of recording devices – something many of these kids may have grown accustom to online. However, as Eric Schmidt predicted, such youthful hijacks will remain available for the world to see and eventually come back to haunt these kids. Unfortunately for some, it came much quicker than expected.

As a result of the Vancouver riots, vigilante websites began to spring up aiming to expose those caught rioting on tape. Captain Vancouver, for instance, started a WordPress blog with the credo that "I'm here to enact and be the judge that will use as my hammer, the historical precedent of public shaming that will ring eternally as long as the internet exists" (publicshamingeternus.wordpress.com/). Captain Vancouver posts photos and video of rioters and seeks to identify them via the rioters' Facebook and social media profiles. If the rioters are not brought to justice, the blog seeks to publically humiliate them, stating "there are failures in our court system especially when dealing with hard to win trials. This shall occur when these rioter's [sic] themselves go on trial and it is why I am moving to publically shame those involved" (publicshamingeternus.wordpress.com/page/3/).

One of the first people exposed by the site was Nathan Kotylak, a 17-year-old Canadian Olympic water polo hopeful, who was shown attempting to light a Police squad car on fire by igniting a shirt sleeve stuffed into the opening of the car's gas tank. After turning himself in to police, Kotylak made an emotional public apology stating that he was provisionally suspended from the National water polo program and that he stands to face charges in court. When asked by a reporter why he did it, Kotylak said "no reasons really" and that he simply "got caught up in the moment" (Global News). Up to that point, Kotylak had no prior criminal charges against him. An interesting aspect of the public apology is that Kotylak's lawyer had to get a court order so that he could be identified; without it, media would not be able to release Kotylak's name or show his face due to his age. When asked why he got a court order to come forward publically, Kotylak stated that the day after the riot, he Googled his name. At that point in time, the top 5 things were all his awards and accomplishments. Four days later, he did the same thing and everything he could find was "some sort of link to what had happened on Wednesday night [the night of the riot]" (Global News). Kotylak felt that his name had been tarnished enough that coming forward was necessary to rebuild his reputation. After the apology, Kotylak's lawyers went on record stating that "the mob mentality that took place at the riots is now happening on social media" (Global Media, June 25 2011).

Kotylak's case and many like his have demonstrated that the line that separates angry mob mentality on the Internet and real life has become blurred. Rioters acted irresponsibly without taking into consideration the long-term impact of their actions – but so too have Internet users and bloggers. Sites like Captain Vancouver's have chosen to disregard Canada's Youth Criminal Justice act which is designed to guarantee that young people's rights are protected, including the right to privacy. The act's publication ban makes it a criminal offense to publish the identity of young offenders including disclosure of their personal information. The act's publication ban "exists to prevent stigmatization of young offenders, which has been found to hinder the rehabilitation of youth" (Bala, 381-388). There will be many rioters who will be convicted of criminal offenses; however, for some offenders, their actions will be stored on servers long after their debt to society has been paid. The interactive ethos of online mob mentality, like the rioters, can lead people to easily get "caught up in the moment" and post and do things that are illegal in Canada.

I do not agree with the riots or destroying public property. As a country with deep civic pride, I can understand why Canadians are upset and wish to bring violators to justice. But we need to ask if anonymously chastising other people online is a healthy and productive response to what the rioters did in Vancouver?

Canada, as a whole, has been granted the opportunity to erase some of the terrible mistakes of its past and reinvent itself. Despite having turned a blind eye to countless Jewish refugees seeking asylum during the Second World War, Canada maintains an identity as an open and peace-loving nation, and rightfully so. The country's commitment to diplomacy, UN peace keeping and multi-culturalism is something to be very proud of. However, whether Canadians and the rest of the world will offer the same opportunity to people like Nathan Kotylak remains to be seen. It could be that online angry mob mentality will prevent such kids from ever having the chance to partake in digital identity rehabilitation. In which case, Eric Schmidt's forecast of young people's digital future is, in my opinion, more frightening and unfortunate than much of what took place during the riots in Vancouver.

Flamebait & the rhetorical hammer of Godwin's Law

Anger can keep you warm at night, and wounded pride can spur a man to wondrous things. – Patrick Rothfuss

In June of 2011, an author by the name of Danny Wind from St. Louis, Missouri managed to piss off most of Belgium with his "children's" book: *Let's Kill All the Belgians: A Child's Guide to Genocide*. Like many people nowadays, Wind did not bother trying to secure a book deal with a title this provocative; rather, he simply found a web-based Print-on-Demand (POD) service to publish and distribute his book for him. Using this approach, users simply go online to order the book and the POD service then prints a copy and ships it directly to the buyer. POD services have become a very popular way for people (including this author), not only to become published authors, but to write about obscure topics for which major publishers would never sign book deals.

It is still unknown as to how the Dutch media got wind (pun intended) of the book, given the massive amount of self-published content available for sale online, but they did. Flemish newspapers such as Het Nieuwsblad (Nieuwsbald.be) and De Morgen (demorgen.de) both ran stories on the book, and shortly thereafter, Internet discussion forums lit up. Calls from Belgium media were made to the author, and even electronic hate mail was sent, as one angry Belgian wrote: "I hate your book 'kill all the Belgians, a child guide for...'. This should be forbidden. Isn't there not enough hate in the world? How should you react if I should tell: 'Let's kill all the US Forces in Irak?'" Misspellings and confusing double negatives aside, were the Belgians correct in voicing their hatred of this book? Should the author have been extradited to The Hague to face charges from the International Court of Justice for crimes against humanity?

While certainly written in poor taste, *Let's Kill All the Belgians: A Child's Guide to Genocide* is satire. It is a 19 page book of poorly drawn images accompanied with simple text. Yes, the book is very inflammatory towards Belgians and certainly provokes a response, stating things like: Belgians will eat your brain; they have no culture; their country smells like pee, and they invented <u>evil</u> Brussels sprouts. But like most children's books, the story has a moral, and in this case, the moral has nothing to do with Belgians and their "smelly" country. In an interview with Flemish newspaper *Flanders Today*, the author states:

> If there's any purpose to the book at all, it's as a parody of a strain in American politics that tends to demonize certain groups (Muslims, Mexican immigrants) without actually knowing anything about them. I picked Belgium because it was about the most inoffensive country I could think of. I thought that would make the joke obvious, since who could actually hate the Belgians? (Hope).

Wind reportedly wrote the book simply to share with his family and friends. If that were the case, he probably should have simply published the book privately using the POD service and just printed a few copies without making it available to the public. However, Wind probably felt no one would notice or, at the very least, most people would recognize the sarcastic tone of the book and realize that it is a joke – something he made note of in the latter half of the book which states:

> *If America's political leaders had any stones at all, they would kill every single Belgian by dropping nuclear bombs on them.*
>
> *But they won't do it, because they are all pussies.*
>
> *But you can change their minds. Write a letter to your Congressman, and ask him not to let Belgians eat your puppy.*
>
> *And take all the money you can find in Mommy and Daddy's wallets and send it with the letter.*

Explain to your classmates about the Belgian threat, and tell them to do the same thing you did.

The politicians will find your arguments so persuasive that they will be convinced to do what must be done about Belgium.

Belgium will be wiped from the face of the Earth.

Once we've killed all the Belgians, you can eat all the ice cream you want, and it will be Christmas every day. Except on your birthday, when it will be Double Christmas. That's right, Double Christmas.

After all the Belgians are dead, then we can get to work on killing all the Swedes.

So if one reads the book, it is pretty clear that Wind is critical of American foreign policy. However, neither the book's cover nor description makes that fact apparent. One has to actually buy and read the book to understand its message. In our instant information world where people are very quick to jump to conclusions and make assumptions, the only things anyone had to reference (in the short term) were the book's cover, title and description – all of which were inflammatory (it should be noted that the author has since added the word "Satire" to the title of the book).

Within the lexicon of online speech, I have to consider Wind's book as flamebait. Flamebait is a term used to describe an inflammatory comment, image, graph, video, blog post or electronic book posted on an online discussion forum that starts a "flame war," i.e., an angry online argument. When people post flamebait, it is almost always intentional, meaning the poster knows that his/her comments will incite anger and does so anyway. From what I understand, Wind did not intentionally set out to start a flame war online, but he had to know that his choice of title was going to piss off a few people – perhaps just not to the extent that it did.

Besides being flamebait, *Let's Kill All the Belgians* is a perfect candidate for testing an online phenomenon known as "Godwin's Law of Nazi Analogies." In a 1994 article in *Wired Magazine*, American attorney and author, Mike Godwin, developed his namesake law based on his observations that "as an online discussion grows longer, the probability of a comparison involving Nazis or Hitler approaches one (100%)" (Godwin, 1). Given enough time, pretty much any online discussion, ranging from cars to chiropractors, will eventually have some sort of argument where someone will make a comparison to Hitler and National Socialism ideology. As Godwin writes,

> In discussions about guns and the Second Amendment, for example, gun-control advocates are periodically reminded that Hitler banned personal weapons. And birth-control debates are frequently marked by pro-lifers' insistence that abortionists are engaging in mass murder, worse than that of Nazi death camps. And in any newsgroup in which censorship is discussed, someone inevitably raises the specter of Nazi book-burning (Godwin, 1).

Regardless of the topic, someone will eventually swing this "handy rhetorical hammer" to help try to end an online debate (Godwin, 1). In July 2011, even well-known bigot Glenn Beck used it when he compared the victims of Norway's mass shooting to "Hitler Youth" (Madison, 1). Given that the book *Let's Kill All the Belgians* involves both genocide and European geo-politics, Godwin's law seemed almost inevitable. And of course, the predictable behavior on online discussion forums did not disappoint. I had no trouble finding online discussions about Wind's book that used Godwin's law. For the sake of brevity, I have selected a single forum discussion that was posted on

Yellows Forum – the unofficial Oxford United Discussion Forum. Oxford United F.C. is an English association football club (soccer for Americans) based in Oxford, UK. I chose this discussion forum because I have studied at Oxford University, and I was pleasantly surprised at their civility – in comparison to other online forums I have read.

The forum discussion, entitled "Lets kill all the Belgians [sic]" begins on June 16, 2011, 11:19 a.m. when "dichio," who reports himself as being male, writes:

> *Lets kill all the Belgians - a childs guide to genocide - is a book that has been written by American author Danny Wild.*
>
> *In the book he says that if all the Belgians are killed everyone can eat ice cream everyday.*
>
> *Asked why he chose the Belgians he replied its because they have no culture and have brought nothing significant to the world.*
>
> *Link to the article (sorry its in french)*
> *http://www.lavenir.net/Article/Detail.aspx?articleID=DMF20110615_00013282*
>
> *I really do despair about the future when i see things like this.* (dichio)

A couple senior members of the discussion forum, those who have made a significant number of posts in the past, are the first to comment on the topic by coming to the defense of the Belgians and their culinary arts (something Wind's book makes fun of):

> *What about moules and really good chips (although they insist on calling them fries).* (sihath)
>
> *bad taste maybe but it is a joke*

> *some of the worlds best beer and chocolate as well* (amarillo)
>
> *....and biscuits. And sprouts. And a language that makes you sound like you have a mouthful of sand.* (yellowhun)

The first female poster, "moobs," joins the conversation, stating:

> *Can you imagine a world without Stella Artois?*
>
> *Stella or Budweiser? No contest....* (moobs)

Yellowhun then raises a good point that should be addressed:

> *Why, if he is American, is it writtten in French?* (yellowhun)

Dichio, the one who started the forum, then posts a link to the article in English and states:

> *The fact that its a childrens book is imo way out of order, the line has to be drawn somewhere.* (dichio)

To which yellowhun replies:

> *.....Yeh, but as you stated earlier - it is written in French. I'm sure the French have far more things to worry about than wiping out the entire Belgian race. (They eat snails you know.)* (yellowhun)
>
> *The original link was the only one i found and written in Belgium hence it being in French, the last link is not in French.*
>
> *Think we should nuke them for eating snails ? Im kinda partial to frogs legs.* (dichio)

> *A small sacrafice to make for eradicating a race of garlic chewing, onion growing, beret wearing nob heads that walk about thinking they are the worlds best lovers. And the women tend to have hairy armpits.* (yellowhun)

Dichio then clarifies whether the book was written in English or French and reaffirms his status as a senior member by keeping the discussion on topic:

> *Sounds like you have enough material to write your own kiddies book.*
>
> *Think we are getting off topic a bit here, the French have nothing to do with this even if the women do have hairy armpits. In Belgium they speak Flemish, French and German. Thats why the original article was in French.* (dichio)
>
> *Well from the little bit I've read it looks pretty sick. Way over the top. But what you have to ask is: Do the American kids reading it have any idea where Belgium is, or even what it is?*
>
> *And there are some lovely things in Belgium: Friets (chips to you), Irene, Chocolates, Josephine, Beer, Karin, the Ardenne, oh and Francine.* (malcolmnl)

Other than Yellowhun's post above that may imply Americans cannot write French, moobs' jab at Budweiser or malcolmnl's post that implies American children do not know their European geography, what follows is the first overt criticism of Americans. I would like to point out that when I studied politics at Oxford, I was amazed at how openly critical our professors and tutors were of Americans. They were not just critical of aggressive US foreign policy; they were critical of America and Americans in general. The same went for students from the UK. So while it may have been warranted at times, I was rather amazed at how critical UK students were of the US. That is probably why someone like jimc is able to make the post below without it back firing or causing much of an issue.

> *I like the last line of the article (written by a Belgian...), which says something like: "Fortunately, as is well known, American children don't know how to read."* (jinc)

Senior Member, "Lone Gunman," whose avatar is a photo of Lee Harvey Oswald's Dallas police mug shot, joins the conversation. He is the first to reply about Americans since Jinc's post, he writes:

> *This reminds me of that american guy who published a book a while back which blamed Britian for all the world's problems, and basically everything bad that has happened in it since about 1600. He even started his own webside and a youtube campaign to create publicity for it as well.* (Lone Gunman)

Enter Paul Cannell, another senior member, who quickly joins the fray:

> *Adolfe Sax, who invented the glockenspiel, was Belgian; and so is Kronenbourg beer.*
>
> *I'm with the Hun on this one, let's kill all the French.* (Paul Cannell)
>
> *Maes and Jupiler deserve honourable mentions. Aside from the populist Stella, Belgium has produced some of the nicest lager in the world.* (unification)
>
> *(quote) Paul Cannell wrote: Adolfe Sax, who invented the glockenspiel, was Belgian; and so is*

> *Kronenbourg beer. I'm with the Hun on this one, let's kill all the French (/quote)*
>
> *The Hun didnt quite get the gist of this thread either, reckon you have been smoking to much Belgian sensimilla. (dichio)*
>
> *Coming to think of it, if they wiped out the EU headquarters in Brussels and all the freeloading Eurocrats within it, like van Rompeuy and the whole gravy train i'd be cheering in the streets.*
>
> *It'd be the same as beating Hitler.... (moobs)*

And there it is, on Jun 16, 2011 at 9:06 p.m., just less than 10 hours after the forum began, the first mention of Hitler appears. The conversation, not all of which I have included here, manages to discuss drugs, alcohol, literacy (or lack thereof), martial arts film stars, Americans, French, Belgians, and Brits before referencing der Führer. Interesting enough, senior member, Maurice Earp, identifies moobs' post as potential flame bait stating:

> *OK, so you're fishing for a reaction I think!*
>
> *You cannot compare this to beating Hitler and no, I don't respect your opinion or thought in this instance.*
>
> *If the Allies had not defeated Hitler I dread to think where the world would be today.* (Maurice Earp)
>
> *It's impossible to tell who's joking and who's not on this thread!* (Young Money)
>
> *That's what Hitler and the Nazis wanted. To unify Europe.*

> *How many British soldiers died for the independence we enjoy today? Now we're giving it up, or I should say Gordon Brown did, and handing all our powers to Brussels.* (moobs).

Replying to Maurice Earp, moob clarifies her unintentional use of Godwin's Law a bit by comparing the Nazi's Lebenstraum campaign with the modern-day European Union, a stretch no doubt. The creator of the thread, dichio, then joins in again to make light of the direction his thread has taken, stating:

> *Well i wasnt but since it descended into a beer and hairy armpit thread with a bit of Hitler thrown in im gonna go with the flow.*
>
> *Reminds me of an exercise we did at school, 30 kids in a circle and the teacher whispers a sentence to the first one who whispers to the next one and so on, by the time it reaches the end it has nothing to do with the original sentence.* (dichio)

Seeing the potential dark path the thread has begun to take, Senior Member "foghornleghorn" joins the conversation with a light-hearted post, perhaps trying to keep the mood civil:

> *The Belgium's invented really big handlebar moustaches. For that we are all in their debt.* (foghornleghorn)

Foghornleghorn's hilarious observation does little to thwart Godwin's Law from spreading. Senior Member, "kidintheriot," lives up to his name by fueling the conversation about Hitler, stating:

> *Didn't hitler want Oxford to play an integral part of ruling Europe? We'd have a cracking football team and wouldn't have had to had dealings with that evil Kassam.* (kidintheriot)

The conversation takes a slight detour as some of the senior members talk about drug use. Amarillo decides to become the voice of reason and prevent the discussion from falling out of control. He writes:

> *(quote) moobs wrote: That's what Hitler and the Nazis wanted. To unify Europe. How many British soldiers died for the independence we enjoy today? Now we're giving it up, or I should say Gordon Brown did, and handing all our powers to Brussels. (/quote)*
>
> *I know you're not being entirely serious, and as pointed out before its hard to tell whos being serious or not on this thread, but its pretty disrespectful to those who died for our independence to compare an organisation run jointly by all the member countries to Hitler wanting to rule over Europe by force.*
>
> *I totally respect sensible arguments against the EU, but there is so much utter bollocks spouted about it, this whole "them" ruling over "us" mentality. The "freeloading eurocrats" might be based in Brussels but they are as much British as they are Belgian...or German, greek whatever. The way some people talk its as if we aren't part of the EU.*
>
> *It should never (even jokingly) be compared to a situation where one country rules over another without its consent and REAL powers are taken away.*
>
> *(This is not a pro-EU argument by the way. Its an argument against the often ridiculous anti-EU sentiment) (Amarillo)*

Moobs, who made the first reference to Hitler, now chimes in again to defend her opinion, stating:

> I won't make any secret of the fact I am completely anti-EU. I don't dislike other Europeans, in fact, I love 'em but the whole EU concept is completely flawed and an utter failure.
>
> The single currency is a complete failure which has now cost our country £22BN in bail outs
>
> Half our MEPs are anti EU which makes you wonder as to the whole point of it?
>
> They keep enforcing barmy laws which are of no benefit or interest to us
>
> Nobody wants it, nobody voted for it, it's just a corrupt gravy train made by politicians for politicians and the sooner the whole experiment goes to the wall and we return to normal the better (moobs)
>
> If nobody wants it why do even the Tories who are eurosceptic like yourself - not pull out? or offer a referendum? (Amarillo)

Perhaps sensing that her argument is not in inline with the thread's majority opinion and thus not likely to get support, moobs chooses not to address amarillo's question and keeps quiet. The discussion then turns to Belgian detective Hercule Poirot and whether he is a better detective than Columbo. The posters encourage others to join the discussion on criminal investigators before one poster mentions "the great Oxford detective, Endeavour Morse." At which point, dichio writes:

> Why would we have mentioned him ? Quite clearly this thread was/is about Killing Belgians, moules frites, Beer, garlic chewing nob heads, the

> *EU, Hitler, sinking the French navy with a catapult, Benny hill, Glockenspeils, sensimilla and songs about a demented milkman. (dichio)*

The conversation continues for at least another two days before growing cold. The full thread can be viewed at the link included at the end of this book (provided it has not been deleted before this book went to print). I chose to end with dichio's statement above because, as the creator of the thread, I thought he did a good job of summing up the discussion. This discussion thread, like countless others online, basically amounts to digital vomit and shows why *Let's Kill All the Belgians: A Child's Guide to Genocide* is flame bait. The book caused a great deal of conversation with no real resolution. People provided their opinions, arguments were had, Hitler and the Nazis were mentioned, pride was wounded, jokes were made and everyone eventually moved on to the next hot topic of the day. All that energy and we are no closer to addressing the central issue of Wind's book – US politics.

As we all know, these types of superfluous online discussions are all around us. This fact leads me to wonder whether meaningful discussions about challenging subjects can be properly addressed online or whether we have simply created an environment where we bicker and annoy one another in loud and heated discussions without offering any kind of solution.

Information overload and the role of bloggers

What the Web 2.0 revolution is really delivering is superficial observations of the world around us rather than deep analysis, shrill opinion rather than considered judgment. - Andrew Keen

I believe that a large part of what makes our current era an age of annoyance is that everyone is seemingly an expert willing to provide their opinions. We are completely inundated with information on a daily basis. We are told conflicting accounts on just about every subject matter – all of which are presented with a great deal of self-appointed authority. To me, the Internet can sometimes feel like that point in an evening when everyone has had too much to drink and we all become professors. We tend to become drunk on our own opinions, something I am not afraid to admit that I have been known to do from time to time myself, both online and off. We make sweeping generalizations and use false analogies without the research or data to support them.

Unfortunately, in such an environment, we can always find websites, infographics, blogs or discussion forums, like Oxford United's Yellows Forum, where like-minded people convene. This has resulted in one of the great ironies of the Internet. While the web gave us all promise of a spectrum of diverse ideas, it has also allowed us to isolate ourselves and simply find corners of the web where our intellectual doppelgängers can reinforce our prejudices and beliefs. Best-selling author and political science professor Thomas Homer-Dixon, sums things up nicely when he writes, "the Internet and the Web – rather than becoming powerful instruments of problem solving, adaptation, and social inclusion – have simply turned into venues for a screaming cacophony of electronic narcissism" (294). We tend to surround ourselves with "communities" that are simply reflections of our own selves. As a result, it has become increasingly hard to remain objective amongst the sheer volume of data online and the isolated online communities we can easily gravitate towards.

Within this new environment, online media has increasingly blurred the distinction between professional and citizen journalists and have, as a result, tested the professional journalist's role of information "gatekeeper" (PEW, 2007, 1). It has become harder nowadays to get a sense of whose information to trust when everyone appears to be an expert online. One has to ask whether bloggers possess the traditional journalistic practices of verification, original sourcing, direct attribution and legal and ethical guidelines (Adams, 2006, 1). Such traits are crucial for reporting the news in an accurate and objective manner – something many bloggers may not exemplify.

Despite our over-crowded media landscape, I tend to believe that there are some bloggers that are in fact more qualified to report the news than many traditionally trained journalists. In 2007, I read a study, Reese et al, that highlights a lack of research on bloggers with different occupational backgrounds. That led me to question whether a lawyer or a researcher with a PHD in economics can report data in an objective, ethical or legal manner just as well as, if not better, than a journalist. I decided to test this theory by examining 60 high-rated political blogs, many of which are run by lawyers, economists, professors, etc, who, for the most part, come from backgrounds other than professional journalism. What I found was that this highly trained and informed group adds diversity to the current media landscape by challenging media frames – in a focused, analytical and well-supported manner. I should point out that while academic training does not necessarily guarantee that one can effectively report news, it does mean that political bloggers, as a group, do possess a degree of expertise not found amongst most journalists, or web communities for that matter.

Before I go any further, I believe some very brief historical context on journalism in this country is in order. Professional journalism has long been considered to be a "restricted practice" (Salter, 1). Whether by professional, technological, economic or political means, the degree to which ordinary citizens were able to participate in news and journalism production in the past had been significantly limited. For the most part, journalism was left to trained professionals. In 1922, Walter Lippman, a young editorial writer at the time, published a book called *Public Opinion,* in which he writes:

> The only hope for effective modern government lay in cultivating a group of well-trained experts, who would manage the country's journalism ... the news papers and magazines produced by these experts would layout conclusions for the public to follow, but no one should expect the public to play more than a passive, spectator's role (Fallow, 236).

Traditionally, the public has had little involvement with news production, and the professionally-trained journalists maintained and enforced a set of professional routines and conventions that are said to "constitute a sort of quality control mechanism in institutional journalism" (Domingo, 12).

While hard to isolate the exact moment when the general public began to take a more active role in journalism, certain events within the last decade show a significant rise in involvement from citizen journalists. It has been argued that the terrorist attacks of September 11, 2001, "were a key moment for the growth of the Internet as a source of news and information" (Trippi, 229). A Pew Research Center Internet study found that in the immediate days after September 11, just three percent of Americans used the Internet as their primary source of news and information. Less than two years later, as the United States was preparing for war with Iraq, that number had grown to 26 percent (Trippi, 229). In just two years, the number of people who used the Internet as a source of news had grown from three percent to more than a fourth of the U.S. population.

Citizen journalists can take on a number of forms. As Joyce Nip writes, citizen journalists can be "one of a number of individuals, a citizen group, or a nonprofit organization without a paid staff running a news blog, new website, community radio station or newspaper" (218). A citizen, or group of citizens, playing an active role in the process of collecting, reporting, analyzing and disseminating news and information can provide, as Shayne Bowman writes, "independent, wide-ranging and relevant information" (5). A 2006 Pew Internet Project (PIP) blogger survey found an increased interest in the practice of blogging.

The report estimated that in 2006 around 12 million American adults kept blogs while 57 million read them (Adams, 2006). According to a 2006 article published in the *Journal of Computer-Mediated Communication*, education proves to be the most significant factor in compelling an Internet user to become a citizen journalist or blogger (Lowrey, 5). As pointed out in the study, higher education levels "lead to an increased confidence in the ability to master the knowledge base of the journalism occupation" (Lowrey, 5). With that said, however, a PEW research study found that most bloggers are focused on describing their personal experiences to a relatively small audience of readers "and that only a small proportion focus their coverage on politics, media, government, or technology" (PEW, 2006, 3). As such, it is important to draw a distinction between the majority of personal blogs that make up the blogosphere, and the small fraction of high-rated political blogs.

With a growing number of citizen journalists posting news and analysis on blogs, one must question the credibility of such news sources and whether or not they are viable alternatives to traditional news sources. Measuring the credibility of blogs proves to be challenging. One feature that some argue may help increase a blogger's credibility is "blogrolling" – or hyperlinking to bloggers' favorite sites. Blogrolling can be used as a credibility assessment component. In this vote-casting system, hyperlinks act as votes, citations, or references to relevant pages on the Web. It can serve as a "web of trust" to mimic the way people share information by word-of-mouth. Credible news blogs often have high blogroll indexes as more web sites and news agencies link to that blog.

For my study, blogrolling played an important role in helping select seemingly more credible political blogs. I began by selecting political blogs that scored high on Google search engine results using the term "political blog." While the exact workings of the Google search algorithm are proprietary information, it is fair to assume that this simple approach would produce accurate results. As the Google Corporate website reports:

> The software behind our search technology conducts a series of simultaneous calculations.

> Traditional search engines rely heavily on how often a word appears on a web page. We use more than 200 signals, to examine the entire link structure of the web and determine which pages are most important. We then conduct hypertext-matching analysis to determine which pages are relevant to the specific search being conducted. By combining overall importance and query-specific relevance, we're able to put the most relevant and reliable results first (google.com/corporate/tech.html).

Given that web-traffic, one can assume, is a part of the Google search algorithm, many of the highest search results were for political blogs associated with mainstream news agencies like the *Washington Post* and *USA Today* whose websites receive very high levels of traffic. Scrolling through the results, I picked blogs that were not associated with mainstream news agencies. After I had picked a blog, I search the blog's "about" or "bio" sections to the blog to get biographical information on the founder or editor of the blog – trying to select those with occupational backgrounds other than professional journalism. Using both information posted on the blogs and Internet searches, I collected education information on the bloggers. While this approach does give rise to false data, I made attempts to match biographical information against multiple online sources. When educational information was not available, I reported the education data as "unknown."

I managed to collect data on 60 bloggers, all of whose blogs scored high in Google search results or were linked to by other high-rated blogs. While this is a limited sample, I feel that it helps prove a point. Based on my initial research, political bloggers without backgrounds in professional journalism and without direct affiliation with mainstream news agencies have high levels of specialized and advanced academic training. Of the 60 bloggers examined, 50 or 83% report having completed undergraduate degrees. Thirty two or 55% have post-graduate degrees, which may include Masters of Arts (MA), Juris Doctor

(JD), Doctor of Philosophy (PHD/DPhil) or Masters of Business Administration (MBA) degrees or Divinity School training. Fourteen or 23% reported having law degrees. Thirteen or 21% reported having PHDs or are PHD candidates. Six or 10% reported having at least three degrees or are working toward a third degree. Ten or 16% did not report having any level of academic training, so it was assumed that they did not have any.

While academic credentials do not necessarily guarantee that one can effectively report news, it does mean that, as a group, political bloggers without backgrounds in professional journalism who are not directly affiliated with mainstream news agencies do, for the most part, provide expert opinions. At the least, these bloggers have a basic level of training in analyzing and reporting facts – common to an undergraduate or post-graduate education.

To examine the role political bloggers play in reporting news, I chose to examine the National Security Agency's (NSA) warrantless surveillance controversy that began under the George W. Bush administration. James Risen and Eric Lichtblau of *The New York Times* broke the story on December 16, 2005 reporting that after the September 11 attacks, President Bush secretly authorized the NSA to eavesdrop on people within the United States to search for evidence of terrorist activity without court-approved warrants. As noted in the article, the legal claim is "whether the surveillance has stretched, if not crossed, constitutional limits on legal searches" (Risen et al, 1). The Bush administration, in a briefing for the press on December 19, 2005 by Attorney General Gonzales and in a subsequent letter to the Intelligence Committees, provides the legal justifications for the NSA program stating that "the President has the inherent authority under the Constitution, as Commander-in-Chief, to engage in this kind of activity" (Smith, 2). On December 22, 2005 the Department of Justice issued a five-page letter outlining its arguments as to why the President's NSA warrantless eavesdropping program was legally justified, stating that "the President has determined that the NSA activities are necessary to the defense of the United States from a subsequent terrorist attack in the armed conflict with al Qaeda" (Moschella, 1). In a 2006 memorandum to the Members of the House Permanent Select

Committee on Intelligence, Jeffrey H. Smith, a former General Counsel of the CIA and a former General Counsel of the Senate Armed Services Committee, stated that,

> On the constitutional point, the President can make a case, although it is weak, that he does have constitutional authority to conduct warrantless wiretaps of American citizens in the U.S. for national security purposes. Because the Supreme Court has never said he does not have this power, some regard it as an open question (2).

The NSA warrantless surveillance controversy provides a solid test case for examining the role bloggers play in reporting the news because it is based on a clear and simple claim made on behalf of the Bush administration, i.e.: the president has authority, and the constitutional obligation to protect U.S. citizens; as such, the NSA surveillance was constitutional and legal. However, because this is a legal, and thus a debatable issue, and because, as Jeffrey Smith points out, the Supreme Court has not said that the president lacks such power, it allows people to challenge the Bush administration's claim from multiple perspectives – legal and otherwise.

Since December 16, 2005, political bloggers have provided a virtual sea of commentary and analysis on whether the NSA program was constitutional and legal. Moreover, because many prominent political blogs are run by lawyers (some of whom practice constitutional law), commentary within the blogosphere was supported, in many cases, by legal claims and precedent. Political blogger Glenn Greenwald claims that "the discussion of the NSA law-breaking scandal in the blogosphere has been infinitely more thorough, informed and informative than in all of the mainstream newspapers, magazines and television programs combined" (January 2006). Surveying all of the data on the NSA warrantless surveillance controversy that is currently available online and comparing it to those of mainstream news agencies, however, is beyond the scope of this book. Moreover, measuring subjective criteria such as whether bloggers are "more thorough, informed and informative" is extremely challenging. So while I think that a strong case can be made to support Greenwald's claim, for the purposes of this book, I have chosen not to ask whether bloggers provided more accurate and thorough reporting on the NSA controversy but whether bloggers were able to provide diversity of coverage by challenging the Bush administration's initial framing of the story, i.e., the NSA surveillance was constitutional and legal?

To answer this question, I have chosen to limit my study to the 60 high-rated political blogs that I have already examined. Of those blogs, I have limited my selection to only the blogs that commented on the NSA surveillance issue within a 2 week period from when the story broke on December 16, 2005 – doing so limits my selection to 25 blogs. While many of the 25 bloggers provided multiple postings on the story within the two week period, I have chosen to simply focus on each blogger's initial blog post on the story. Doing so will help one get a sense of whether the bloggers were either critical, supportive or indifferent to the Bush administration's claim that the warrantless surveillance program was constitutional and legal. Moreover, the study also lists the evidence each blogger used, or did not use, to support their claims.

Of the 25 blogs examined, the majority was overwhelmingly critical of the Bush administration and challenged its claim that the NSA warrantless surveillance program was constitutional and legal. The second highest majority was those who were impartial of the Bush administration. This group neither criticized nor defended the Bush administration's claim directly. Rather they chose to remain somewhat unbiased towards the claim until more information became available. There were also those who were critical of *The New York Times* for running the article – but for different reasons. As noted in the December 16, 2005, Risen & Lichtblau article,

> The White House asked *The New York Times* not to publish this article, arguing that it could jeopardize continuing investigations and alert would-be terrorists that they might be under scrutiny. After meeting with senior administration officials to hear their concerns, the newspaper

delayed publication for a year to conduct additional reporting (1).

Blogger Glenn Greenwald argues that, "there is absolutely no justification at all for the *Times* covering up these illegal acts on the part of the Government for a full year" (December 17, 2005, 1). For Greenwald, the *Times* had a journalistic obligation to inform the public. Conversely, the blogs "Little Green Footballs," "Powerline," and "Right-Wing Nut House" were critical of *The New York Times* for jeopardizing national security by running the story – claiming that the *Times* put newspaper sales ahead of national security.

The most obvious and striking finding is that, despite differing opinions, none of the bloggers initially defended the Bush administration's claim that the NSA warrantless surveillance program was constitutional and legal. This could be the result of the types of blogs that were used in my study. However, there were numerous well-known Republican blogs that were examined. As one Republican blogger wrote:

> Some of my very good Republican friends may wonder why I am so passionately opposed to the administration on these sorts of questions, and I would respond that the reason I feel so strongly is because of the precedent that it sets. If a Republican administration can circumvent the Constitution to apprehend terrorists, than any future administration can do the same to any person or people it deems a threat to itself (Oatney, 1).

In the wake of *The New York Times* article, suspicions amongst both Democrats and Republicans were raised as to the legality of the Bush administrations "secret" NSA program, and it appears that most people were reluctant to support it openly from the onset. Rather, bloggers chose to either challenge the claim directly, question it, or focus attention away from the Bush administration and towards *The New York Times*. It is my assumption that some felt they could criticize the *Times* because deciding to print the story was a matter of principle, and principles, unlike legal claims, are more subjective – thus requiring less stringent legal justification and research to support one's claim. As such, most, if not all, of the bloggers who were either critical or impartial towards the Bush administration backed their claims with some sort of evidence.

Regardless of whether they were critical or impartial towards the Bush administration, 92% of the blogs studied supported their claims by citing: other news sources, legal grounds, legal precedent, political precedent, or opinions of Senate leaders. One blogger backed his claim with his personal opinion while another stated that more data was needed before making a judgment.

While opinions varied, bloggers not only challenged the claims of the Bush administration, they made attempts to back their claims with substance. Of the 25 bloggers examined, only one backed his claim with his personal opinion as opposed to citing other news sources or legal grounds. I believe that it is fair to argue, therefore, that political bloggers added diversity to the debate as to whether the NSA surveillance program was constitutional and legal by not only challenging the Bush administration's claim, but, for the most part, by also supplying meaningful data to add to the overall debate about the issue.

Because of their role in challenging the Bush administration's claim, the mainstream media often turned to bloggers for information on the NSA warrantless surveillance program. Perhaps the most famous example of a blogger receiving national media attention on the NSA surveillance program was Glenn Greenwald. On January 24, 2006 in a blog post entitled "The Administration's new FISA defense is factually false," Greenwald argues that even while the Bush administration had begun its warrantless eavesdropping, the Department of Justice expressed serious doubts about the program's constitutionality. As Greenwald writes, "the DoJ was concerned that it might be unconstitutional to eavesdrop with a lower standard than probable cause *even as the Administration was doing exactly that"* (January 24, 2006). To support his claim, Greenwald makes reference to statements made in 2002 by the Bush administration in response to Republican Senator Michael DeWine of Ohio, who had proposed an easier standard for domestic eavesdropping by federal agents. The Administration had declined any interest in the legislation and advised DeWine that it would more than likely be an unconstitutional act – a complete contradiction to the rationale which would later be used by the Administration to justify the NSA warrantless spying. Front-page articles appeared in the *Washington Post*, the *Los Angeles Times* and other newspapers, all of which credited Greenwald's blog for the story. *Washington Post* writer Dan Eggen, in an article entitled "White House Dismissed '02 Surveillance Proposal," writes: "The DeWine amendment [is] the latest point of contention in a fierce political and legal battle over the NSA monitoring program, [it was] first highlighted ... by Internet blogger Glenn Greenwald and widely publicized yesterday by the Project on Government Secrecy, an arm of the Federation of American Scientists" (1).

The debate as to the legality of the NSA surveillance program also took place outside of the blogosphere and mainstream media. On February 9, 2006, leading law experts from universities such as Duke, Yale, Harvard, Georgetown and NYU wrote a letter in *The New York Review of Books* entitled "On NSA Spying: A Letter to Congress." In the letter, they write:

> We are scholars of constitutional law and former government officials. We write in our individual capacities as citizens concerned by the Bush administration's National Security Agency domestic spying program. One of the crucial features of a constitutional democracy is that it is always open to the President—or anyone else—to seek to change the law. But it is also beyond dispute that, in such a democracy, the President cannot simply violate criminal laws behind closed doors because he deems them obsolete or impracticable (Bradley, 1).

The authors of the letter, like the bloggers studied here, backed their claims with numerous well-supported legal arguments and legal precedent. I chose to include this letter because it helps support the claims of those political bloggers who were critical of the Bush administration's warrantless surveillance. Moreover, it demonstrates how concerned citizens were able to join the debate outside of the blogosphere. Whether or not the bloggers who challenged the Bush administration encouraged other people to join the debate is perhaps worth further investigation.

In August 2006, the first federal challenge ever argued against the President's NSA spying program took place with the case of the American Civil Liberties Union (ACLU) vs. the National Security Agency (NSA). In the case, U.S. District Court Judge Anna Diggs Taylor ruled that the NSA program violates the First Amendment, the Fourth Amendment, and the Foreign Intelligence Surveillance Act. In her decision, Judge Taylor writes, "it was never the intent of the Framers to give the President such unfettered control ... particularly where his actions blatantly disregard the parameters clearly enumerated in the Bill of Rights" (aclu.org, 1). In July 2007, the 6th Circuit overturned Judge Taylor's decision. After that, the ACLU, on behalf of prominent journalists, scholars, attorneys and national nonprofit organizations, asked the Supreme Court of the United States to consider the ruling; but in February 2008, the Court declined to review the challenge (aclu.org). In August 2008, the United States Foreign Intelligence Surveillance Court of Review (FISCR) affirmed the constitutionality of the Bush administration's "Protect America Act of 2007" in an opinion released on January 15, 2009. James Risen and Eric Lichtblau, the two *New York Times* writers who originally broke the NSA surveillance story, write:

> But the ruling, handed down in August 2008 by the Foreign Intelligence Surveillance Court of Review and made public Thursday, did not directly address whether President Bush was within his constitutional powers in ordering domestic wiretapping without warrants, without first getting Congressional approval, after the terrorist attacks of 2001. William C. Banks, a law professor at Syracuse University who has criticized the administration's legal position on eavesdropping, said that while the ruling did not address Mr. Bush's surveillance without warrants directly, "it does bolster his case" by recognizing

that eavesdropping for national security purposes did not always require warrants (January 15, 2009, 1).

So while the Bush administration has won legal battles to support its claim, the original question remains unanswered. Does the President have the constitutional power to order surveillance without warrants? Until the question goes before the Supreme Court, it will more than likely remain, as Jeffrey Smith writes, "an open question" for informed citizens to respond to, either through weblogs, the media or other means (2).

As we all know, the number of people keeping blogs online and offering their opinions on discussion forums have risen dramatically over the past decade. Many people question both blogger's and regular citizen's abilities to report news in an objective and critical manner – leading to a growing perception that blogs and websites not affiliated with traditional news outlets are unreliable sources of information. However, while the vast majority of blogs and websites are simply personal web journals posted to a small group of people, within the blogosphere there is a group of highly trained and qualified experts commentating on political news. Political bloggers without backgrounds in professional journalism and who are not directly affiliated with mainstream news agencies have high levels of specialized and advanced academic training. As exhibited by the coverage of the Bush administration's NSA warrantless surveillance controversy, political bloggers are able to provide diversity of coverage by challenging media frames with in-depth, critical and well-supported analysis.

In an age of annoyance where we are bombarded with information, it is refreshing to see that there are those who are providing more than just "shrill opinions" on important subjects. Political bloggers are able to examine issues from multiple perspectives and challenge claims made in the media. Diversity of perspective should remain a vital part of journalism, the future of news media, and the future of Internet discourse. Within our overcrowded media landscape, however, it is up to the end user to seek out these truly qualified experts – a task that may only become more challenging with time as more people continue to express their "expert" views online.

Maintaining the appearance of control

In this curious relational space, even sophisticated users who know that electronic communications can be saved, shared, and show up in court, succumb to its illusion of privacy. – Sherry Turkle

In late March of 2011, Epsilon, the leading provider of multi-channel marketing services sending over 40 billion emails each year to over 2,500 clients, experienced a massive security breach (White). Companies like TiVo, Disney, and Best Buy were all affected. Even if you have never heard of Epsilon or do not know what they do, chances are you are a subscriber to one of their many big named clients' eNewsletters, and you may have received an email in your inbox similar to the ones below:

> From: **Walgreens** <Walgreens@email.walgreens.com>
> Date: Mon, Apr 4, 2011 at 8:17 PM
> Subject: A Message from Walgreens
>
> Dear Valued Customer,
>
> On March 30th, we were informed by Epsilon, a company we use to send emails to our customers, that files containing the email addresses of some Walgreens customers were accessed without authorization.
>
> We have been assured by Epsilon that the only information that was obtained was your email address. No other personally identifiable information was at risk because such data is not contained in Epsilon's email system.
>
> For your security, we encourage you to be aware of common email scams that ask for personal or sensitive information. Walgreens will not send you emails asking for your credit card number,

social security number or other personally identifiable information. If ever asked for this information, you can be confident it is not from Walgreens.

We regret this has taken place and any inconvenience this may have caused you. If you have any questions regarding this issue, please contact us at 1-855-814-0010. We take your privacy very seriously, and we will continue to work diligently to protect your personal information.

Sincerely,

Walgreens Customer Service Team

Copyright 2010 Walgreen Co., 200 Wilmot Road, Deerfield, IL 60015-4620. All rights reserved.

From: Marriott <Marriott@marriott-email.com>
Date: Tue, Apr 5, 2011 at 7:45 PM
Subject: Important Notice from Marriott International, Inc.

April 4, 2011

Dear Marriott Customer,

We were recently notified by Epsilon, a marketing vendor used by Marriott International, Inc. to manage customer emails, that an unauthorized third party gained access to a number of Epsilon's accounts including Marriott's email list.

In all likelihood, this will not impact you. However, we recommend that you continue to be on the alert for spam emails requesting personal or sensitive information. Please understand and be assured that Marriott does not send emails requesting customers to verify personal information.

We take your privacy very seriously. Marriott has a long-standing commitment to protecting the privacy of the personal information that our guests entrust to us. We regret this has taken place and apologize for any inconvenience.

Please visit our FAQ to learn more.

Sincerely,

Marriott International, Inc.

Marriott- Internet Customer Care
1818 North 90 Street
Omaha, NE 68114-1315 USA

©2011 Marriott International

Given the scale of the security breach, I have to give credit to Epsilon for addressing the issue as quickly as they did. By providing a boilerplate that could easily be reused by their clients, end users where quickly notified on how to identify potential phishing scams – attempts to acquire sensitive data by masquerading as a trusted source, something that happens after large breaches such as these.

The Epsilon breach sent shockwaves through the email marketing community, as marketing professionals began to anticipate the fallout from such a large scale hack. Joe Colopy, the CEO of Bronto Software which offers similar solutions to Epsilon, conveyed an interesting assessment of the Epsilon breach on his blog. Colopy begins his post by making reference to a famous bank robber, Willie Sutton, who when asked by a reporter why he robs banks, Sutton replied "because that's where the money is"

(Colopy, 1). In an era where identifiable information is a valuable form of currency, Email Service Providers who control massive reserves of it, Colopy argues, "are the new banks" (Colopy, 1). Partly to reassure confidence in his own clients, Colopy does address the need for ESPs to ramp up their security and allow their clients greater control over the safety of their data.

The Epsilon data breach was potentially damaging enough that US Senators and House members demanded that Epsilon and its parent company, Alliance Data, disclose the number of customers impacted and how the breach happened. In an April 6 letter to the United States Attorney General's Office, U.S. Senator Richard Blumenthal of Connecticut writes: "while some of Epsilon's client companies have notified their customers of the breach, other consumers may be unaware that their names, email addresses and other potentially identifying information may be at risk" (Rashid, 1). Given that neither Social Security numbers nor credit card information was included within the breach, state laws that require people to be notified may not apply in this particular case. Epsilon did not release the number of affected accounts from the breach and simply posted on their website that:

> Information that was obtained was limited to email addresses and/or customer names only. A rigorous assessment determined that no other personal identifiable information associated with those names was at risk. A full investigation is currently underway (Epsilon, April 1, 2011).

How the breach took place may have been much simpler than one would expect. Given that Epsilon was tightlipped about the nature of the breach directly after it happened, news agencies were stuck having to seek the advice of security experts to determine possible vulnerabilities in Epsilon's network. *Fast Company*, for instance, contacted phishing expert Jason Hong, a computer scientist at Carnegie Mellon who put forth numerous possibilities; he states:

> It might be "script kiddies" (amateur hackers out for fun or bragging rights), or it might be more sophisticated hackers who want email addresses for spamming purposes. Or it could be a rival of Epsilon out to embarrass them. It's also possible that hackers thought there was more information on Epsilon's servers, but didn't find anything interesting (Zax, 1).

I tend to believe that the simplest explanation is, more often than not, the most correct. The most concise explanation I have heard of how the Epsilon breach could have taken place was from Bronto CEO Joe Colopy at an email marketing conference.

Joe noted that, not surprisingly, these types of breaches are done by networks of highly organized groups. Somewhat surprisingly, however, is that social engineering actually plays a key role in such breaches. The hackers will search online and target a high-profile or super user in an organization – sometimes with just a simple Google search. For Epsilon, it may have been a Director of Client Services, or someone who would have been granted high access user log-in privileges but may not have been as cognizant of security issues as a Network Administrator or Security Director. Once said person was identified, the hackers would send this person some form of malicious keystroke logging malware that records the user's keyboard stokes. From there, the hackers could decipher the keystrokes used for the user's username and password. After which point, they could log-in and set-up another super-user account with an unknown username and password and begin exporting data. While this may NOT have been the case with Epsilon, such an approach would be simple and highly effective. From a network security standpoint, a company like Epsilon could prevent such attacks from happening by locking-down access to accounts that export large amounts of data (particularly on holiday weekends), prevent or restrict remote VPN log-in to company networks or restrict it to certain IP addresses, and prevent super-user accounts from having access to multiple client sub-accounts.

On June 29, 2011 Epsilon sent out a press release entitled "Epsilon Unveils Innovative Security Enhancements to Global Email Marketing Platform." The updated security solutions outlined within the press release leads me to believe that Colopy was correct in his assessment of how the breach took place. As Epsilon stated in the release:

> Epsilon has instituted stringent new access restrictions through its IP certification requirements. All access to the email platform, both inbound and outbound, will be restricted to white-listed IP addresses. Further, Epsilon has enhanced user security by implementing two-factor authentication. Two-factor authentication is a security process that requires two means of identification to gain system access, adding significant additional protections beyond conventional strong password requirements. Two-factor authentication, currently in place for employees, will be extended to all clients in Q3 2011 (Epsilon.com, 1).

To me, the above solutions point to the cause of the problem. Someone from an outside IP range used an employee's account to gain access to the Epsilon system. Epsilon has fixed the problem by only allowing trusted IPs to access their network resources. Moreover, employee and client log-in access will have a greater level of authentication moving forward. While it was an unfortunate incident, I have to give a great deal of credit to Epsilon for how the company handled the situation. They took ownership of the breach and provided, while over 90 days later, viable solutions to the issue.

I chose to use the Epsilon data breach to highlight a point I think is crucial for effective communication in our digital world – namely the importance of maintaining the appearance of control. Right after the breach, Epsilon provided a statement that clients could use to send to their end users. They worked with authorities to find the causes of the breach and then sent a press release stating their solutions to the problem. In short, they took responsibility for a problem quickly, but more importantly, they gave the appearance that they were in control of the situation. I have no idea if Epsilon has lost clients over the breach. At the time of writing this book, Alliance Data (ADS on NYSE) had not release their quarterly earnings for Q2 2011. However, ADS' stock has been on an upward trend ever since the breach. With time, we will get a better sense of the financial costs of this breach, but for now, I am more interested in asking whether the Epsilon breach will change how we view Internet security and our individual online data? Personally, I really do not think it will.

So long as there is the appearance of control, we really do not care that much about our personal data online. All of our information, both social and financial, is hosted online in the cloud. In his book *The Information,* James Gleick writes, "All traditional ideas of privacy, based on doors and locks, physical remoteness and invisibility, are upended in the cloud" (396). He continues by stating:

> Money lives in the cloud: the old forms are vestigial tokens of knowledge about who owns what, who owes what. To the twenty-first century these will be seen as anachronisms, quaint or even absurd: bullion carried from shore to shore in fragile ships, subject to the tariffs of pirate and the god Poseidon; mental coins tossed from moving cars into baskets at highway tollgates and thereafter trucked about (now the history of your automobile is in the cloud); paper checks torn from pads and signed in ink; tickets for trains, performances, air travel, or anything at all, printed on weighty perforated paper with watermarks, holograms, or fluorescent fibers; and, soon enough, all forms of cash. The economy of the world is transacted in the cloud (396).

If we really cared about the security of our online personal data, wouldn't we do a much greater job of protecting it? We get upset when a company like Epsilon gets hacked, but we freely hand over our data to them. We enable cookies and save passwords within our browser and do not realize that dynamic retargeting companies like FetchBack® can serve up targeted advertisements long after we have left a website; i.e., you go to a website, window shop and leave that site, cookie information stored in your browser serves up an advertisement for that same company later in your web browsing on an entirely different site. Put another way, advertisers follow you as you surf the Internet based on the trail of cookie crumbs you leave online. Flash-based "Supercookies" are now also being used by major retailers that are almost impossible for computers to detect. While you may feel you have control over what you do online, behind your browser in lines of code are countless bits of personalized data being shared with third-party companies. None of us has control over our data in the cloud and it is important to remember that such data "is stored on servers most of us don't own" (Freeman, 128). We grant access to our personal information to countless sites online because such companies are able to maintain the appearance of control. Sure, there are plenty of companies with incredible network security features, but at the same time, there are those who can potentially hack massive amounts of data with very basic means. It is not until something goes wrong, a system gets hacked or something breaks down, that we cry foul and take interest in our personal online data again. Yes, we are correct for blaming companies when such things happen but there is a level of responsibility on the part of the end user that we need to remember to address whenever possible.

We're all lazy until the machine stops

Software can end up turning the most intimate and personal activities into mindless rituals [where] rather than acting according to our own knowledge and intuition ... we cede control over the flow of our thoughts and memories to a powerful electronic system. - Nicholas Carr

In college, I wrote a screenplay around the time of Y2K. If you remember, that was when everyone was worried about an impending digital Armageddon known as the millennium bug. Our over-dependence on technology was to come crashing down as major computer systems fumbled to comprehend the new date rollover from 99 to 00. This threat compelled me to imagine a similar crisis a couple hundred years in the future when every aspect of our lives would be completely automated – not just bathroom sinks, toilets and doors – I mean everything! Room temperature would be controlled automatically by your body temperature. Your car (or transportation device) would start as soon as you approached it. Your fridge would be automatically stocked based on your previous consumption preferences, etc, etc, etc. Now imagine children born into this world, aka hyper digital natives. What incentive would such children have to figuring out how everything works, when everything already works exactly as it is supposed to?

We have all heard of "flow," or as the Chinese Taoist Philosophers call it *Wu-Wei*. It is when you do something repetitively enough that you no longer notice that you are doing it. Athletes and musicians easily fall into a state of flow after years of training. I go Wu-Wei, for instance, when I commute to work each morning, provided there are no distracting accidents or traffic jams. Highway hypnosis sets in and I no longer feel like I am driving. Before I know it, I am at work.

In my screenplay, I imagined a world where everything is fully automated; the children born into such a society live in a permanent state of technology-governed flow. Doors open, cars start, groceries appear, all with seamless precision and accuracy.

A bi-product of such a state of being is that children unknowingly develop a false sense of telekinesis. They believe that it is their minds that open the door, start the car, and stock the fridge.

The story revolves around how different characters deal with the crushing reality that their supposed sixth sense never existed. Some technological disaster takes place (similar to Y2K) and things no longer work as they are supposed to. Like someone losing their eye sight, just getting out of bed or getting dressed becomes a major challenge. For some of the people in the story, the experience is frightening. For others, it is liberating. But for all of the characters, there is some level of rage and frustration as tasks that are supposed to be easy become exceedingly difficult.

When I pitched the screenplay to a local film producer, he informed me that the story had already been written almost 90 years prior. *The Machine Stops* is a science fiction short story by E. M. Forster. Like my screenplay, it is a story about man's overdependence on technology. While it is an excellent story and it is very impressive that Forster was able to correctly anticipate things like television and videoconferencing, I feel that *The Machine Stops* does not accurately capture our current reliance on technology.

Forster assumes that people will not be exceedingly lazy in the future. In the story, Forster talks about "the Book of the Machine." He writes, "in it were instructions against every possible contingency. If she was hot or cold or dyspeptic or at a loss for a word, she went to the book, and it told her which button to press" (7). In Forster's world, technology is not fully automated; one still has to consult a very large book to find the answer to a problem and actually hit a physical button to make the technology work.

My feeling is that consulting a very large instruction manual made sense to the people living in Forster's time. Sears, Roebuck and Co., for instance, constructed a forty-acre $5 million mail-order plant and office in Chicago in 1906. From that location the company was able to produce a truly remarkable product – the 786 page *1897 Sears Wish Book*. Crammed into something the size of a phone book, author Chris Anderson writes, "are 200,000 items and variations, all described with tiny type and some 6,000 lithographic illustrations … [t]his was mind-blowing stuff for a rural farm family" (43). This reference guide allowed farmers to have access to an incredible array of new technologies. All a person would have to do is open the book, reference the index, find the product they were looking for and order it. "The Machine"(in this case the railroad system) and Sears, Roebuck and Co. (the distribution network) would handle the rest.

Unfortunately, such an approach is too labor intensive in today's technology-driven society. When the Yellow Pages arrive on my doorstep, I throw it directly into the recycling bin. It is useless, as far as I am concerned. If I am hungry and want to find a place close-by to eat, I can check Yelp™ on my iPhone or just Google "Mexican Food." I don't even need to put in my location; my device's geolocation is already captured and I am given a host of options all with reviews and contact information right at my fingertips. People naturally seek out those software tools and websites, Nicholas Carr writes, "that offer the most help and the most guidance – and shun those that are difficult to master" (217). We want friendly, helpful software. One of my co-workers said to me that an iPad is more intuitive than spelling, meaning that his three year old could figure how to operate games and videos on a tablet before he could spell. That is the way humans expect machines to be.

Today, we buy cars that parallel park themselves and we use software that auto-corrects the words we mistype. We don't want to read instruction manuals – particularly ones that resemble giant books. If someone cannot show us how to do it or if we cannot watch a short how-to commercial, we will continue to demand products that are intuitive enough that we don't need to figure them out. Essentially, we want products that we can operate out-of-the-box.

Getting back to Forster's story, I do agree with his predictions for how people would handle themselves when technology breaks down. We only love technology when it works and go crazy when it doesn't. In Forster's world, the omnipresent Machine is worshipped as a god. The Machine, Forster writes, "is omnipotent, eternal; blessed is the Machine." (25). The Machine clothes people, houses them and through it people speak and see one another. It is a blessed caregiver whose status has even made it a substitute for religion. When the Machine eventually breaks down, however, panic reigns supreme. As Forster writes,

> Others were yelling for Euthanasia or for respirators, or blaspheming the Machine. Others stood at the doors of their cells fearing, like herself, either to stop in them or to leave them. And behind all the uproar was silence - the silence which is the voice of the earth and of the generations who have gone (29- 30).

In Forster's story, the earth watches in silent indifference as humanity falls to its peril, having long ago put its faith in a Demigod that eventually stops operating. After which time, humanity has nothing but disdain for the thing it once loved. While falling to their deaths, humanity projects its anger on the Machine because it is much easier to blame an object then it is to blame oneself. Taking out our frustrations on machines, whether within an angry email reply or just saying "you stupid computer," is something that plagues all of us today, and it is something Forster anticipated extremely well.

The Spazz

We have met the Devil of Information Overload and his impish underlings, the computer virus, the busy signal, the dead link, and the PowerPoint presentation. – James Gleick

When we freak out on machines, it is something I refer to as "the Spazz." The Spazz has nothing to do with the German word for fun or enjoyment – *Spaß* (spass). In fact, it is quite the opposite. It is an overly-dramatic reaction: another way to describe a major freak out over something trivial.

At one time or another, we have all experienced The Spazz – even Germans. If you are reading this book electronically, stop what you are doing and Google "angry German kid." Chances are, you have already seen the video, as it has become extremely popular over the years. If you haven't, it is a YouTube video of a portly child who looks like *Willie Wonka's* Augustus Gloop experiencing a complete and utter meltdown which I would certainly describe as the opposite of fun or enjoyment. The young boy, who has been referred to as Leopold, sits at his computer to play the video game Unreal Tournament, but as his computer loads too slowly for his liking, he smashes his keyboard and swears at his computer screen. Researching this story online seems to have infested my computer with spyware and viruses for most of the websites and blog posts that have commented on this story are of ill-repute. I would, therefore, caution you to take any facts about this story with a grain of salt.

Apparently, the viewer is meant to believe that the Leopold's dad secretly set-up a web camera to capture his child's out-of-control behavior and addiction to online video games. But many commentators seem to think the video was staged and meant to be a satirical commentary on Germany's "Killerspiel Debatte" – a debate similar to those within the United States about the impact of video game violence on children. Whether the video is real or staged is irrelevant in my eyes. Its popularity is due to the fact that (a) it is hilarious and (b) it is an exaggerated version of something that anyone with a computer and Internet connection has experienced at one time or another – the Spazz.

The age of annoyance – interruptions

Things that keep us from accomplishing a task are annoying. -
Flora Lichtman & Joe Palca

Annoyances are extremely subjective. Something that you might find annoying, I may actually find quite enjoyable. Take this hypothetical situation for instance. Two people live together. One person gets extremely annoyed when the other watches documentaries on the History channel. While one hates such programs, the other person could easily spend an entire afternoon watching WW2 in HD. Watching shows on the Food Network, on the other hand, is what the first person looks forward to. In this example, both roommates share the same annoyance – the only difference is their TV viewing preferences. If either person were living alone, they would have no reason to dislike the History channel or the Food Network, respectively. Each would just choose never to watch the disliked channel, and it would simply fade back into obscurity along with the thousands of other channels Time Warner Cable® provides each day. But when the roommates are together, the History channel is something that prevents the other from watching the Food Network. The History channel thus becomes an interruption – something that clogs up the DVR and prevents optimum television viewing. So while they have different TV preferences, the roommates are both annoyed by interruptions. To remain happily living together, both roommates avoid such interruptions by finding programs they both like (Mad Men, Survivor, 30 Rock) and leave the documentaries and cooking shows for times when only one of them is around and is free to watch what either wants to watch – interruption free – thus avoiding annoyance.

As a society of digital multi-taskers, we are constantly being interrupted. The minute we turn on our computer or mobile device we inhabit, as Cory Doctorow writes, an "ecosystem of interruption technologies … [where] anything that leaps up on your screen to announce something new, occupies your attention" (1). Instant messages, RSS updates, emails, News feeds, and Twitter updates – they are all interruption technologies designed to make their presence known and, whether on a conscious or subconscious level, we are compelled to deal with them as soon as possible. In 2001, a study by the University of Minnesota Department of Computer Science and Engineering investigated such online interruptions on 50 subjects. The study used two categories of peripheral information (i.e., distractions) – breaking news headlines and stock market updates – while the subjects were involved in performing primary work-related tasks. A user from either of the two groups, a control and experimental group, performed eighteen primary tasks, three from each of six task categories. A user from the control group was presented with a peripheral task just after completing two of three primary tasks in each category, while a user from the experimental group was interrupted during two of three primary tasks in each category. In both conditions, the user attended to the peripheral task immediately (Bailey et al, 2). While this description of the experiment has probably already confused you as much as it did me, the key findings of the study are:

> (i) a user performs slower on an interrupted task than a noninterrupted task, (ii) the level of annoyance experienced by a user depends on both the category of primary task being performed and the time at which a peripheral task is displayed, (iii) a user experiences a greater increase in anxiety when a peripheral task interrupts her primary task than when it does not, and (iv) a user perceives an interrupted task to be more difficult to complete than a noninterrupted task (Bailey et al, 2).

The timing of distraction and the importance of the primary task seem to be two strong factors in the level of annoyance one experiences. That should not come as much of a surprise to most people. If it is 8:55 a.m. and you are at the photo copy machine rushing to make print-outs for a 9:00 a.m. meeting with your boss, and a colleague comes to chat about your weekend plans, that is potentially an annoying interaction that would be better saved for later in the day. That is why, as the study points out,

> Waiting for an opportune moment before interrupting someone's task is a social behavior commonly found in human-human interaction. Interrupting a person who is visibly concentrating on a task, except in the most extreme circumstances, is considered rude and socially unacceptable behavior, as it disrupts that person's concentration (Bailey et al, 1).

The authors of the study also argue that socially unacceptable behavior also pertains to machines, stating that "it is equally rude and distracting for an automating application to unnecessarily interrupt a user's current task" (Bailey et al, 1). When building computer applications, one should be mindful of when and how users are interrupted – if at all. Microsoft Office, for instance, should avoid sending a pop-up notifying you that your computer needs to shut down in order to load a software update while you are creating year-end Excel reports for the next day's Board of Director's meeting. But why it insists on doing so, I have no idea. As a recommendation for developers, the authors of the study introduce the idea of an "attention manager" that "would first observe or predict an opportune moment for gaining user attention and then notify the next waiting application" (Bailey et al, 8).

All good email marketers practice what could be called proper attention management forecasting. Marketers deploy messages to people at different times of the day and collect data as to when an end user is most likely to open or click-thru an email message. Ask any email marketer and s/he will have different statistical analysis on the optimum time of day for sending emails. One option is to target the "bored at work crowd" (BAWC). The BAWC are the folks who have just returned from lunch and are not quite ready to get back to work. They have had the morning to clear out their inboxes and now just want to relax for a bit. They will use the time to forward a hilarious YouTube video of a baby monkey riding backwards on a pig to friends or take the time to book a well-deserved pedicure for after work. If there is ever a time to dish up some email Bacn, it is now. The chances of you interrupting a "primary task" are low, as is your likelihood of initiating annoyance.

The BAWC can also extend into what I call the 2:30 doldrums. Marketers know all too well about this idle time of inactivity. I am sure you have seen the 5-hour energy ad campaign: "You Know What 2:30 in the Afternoon Feels Like, Right?" The advertisement shows a well-dressed narrator walking through a stereotypical office space where groggy and slow moving employees struggle to stay awake. Instead of grabbing a soda or coffee, the narrator encourages buyers to take a 5-hour energy and see what the rest of your day feels like. The camera then cuts to a shot of active office employees where the narrator concludes the commercial by stating that with 5-hour energy your afternoon "sure won't feel like 2:30 anymore." Similarly, in a Super Bowl ad, Emerald Nuts did a more comical take on the same theme. The commercial begins by stating that around 3:00 p.m. when one's blood-sugar and energy are low, Robert Goulet appears and messes with your stuff. Goulet shreds your work documents, dances on your desk, and kicks over your pens. But the natural energy of just one handful of Emerald Nuts "is enough to keep Robert Goulet away…until tomorrow anyway."

In an age of annoyance, forecasting the best times to interrupt someone is key for both marketers and the general public. We want to be mindful of when and where we can interrupt primary tasks so as not to be seen as annoying Robert Goulets who mess with people's stuff.

The age of annoyance – speed & convenience

We are addicted to speed and convenience for the sake of speed and convenience. – Siva Vaidhyanathan

So while timing is important for minimizing annoyance, so too is speed. I would argue that speed, particularly a lack thereof, is one of the most annoying aspects of the Internet. Whether we are involved in performing a primary task or just wanting to kill our friends while playing Unreal Tournament, slow load times give rise to those unpleasant mental states of irritation and distraction which lead to emotions such as frustration and anger. At the 2011 Bronto Summit, a conference for email marketers, keynote speaker Suchirita Mulpuru, Vice President and Principal Analyst of Forrester Research, noted that "47% of consumers expect a page to load in less than 2 seconds" (Bronto Summit). During a 2008 keynote speech at a software developer's conference, Google's Vice President Marissa Mayer stated that "one of the most significant things that Google discovered in its early user studies was that speed mattered more than anything else in generating a 'positive user experience'" (Vaidhyanathan, 53 - 54). It should come as no surprise that people demand speed on the Internet.

In February of 2011, Cisco released its "Visual Network Index: Global Mobile Data Traffic Forecast Update, 2010-2015" report and subsequent marketing campaigns. Cisco reports that:

> Globally, the average mobile network connection speed in 2010 was 215 kbps. The average speed will grow at a compound annual growth rate of 60 percent, and will exceed 2.2 Mbps in 2015. Smartphone speeds, generally 3G and higher, are currently nearly five times higher than the overall average. Smartphone speeds will quadruple by 2015, reaching 4.4 Mbps (12).

A subheading of Cisco's report is called "ubiquitous mobility." The company forecasts exponential growth in the use of mobile devices. Global mobile data traffic "nearly tripled (2.6-fold growth) in 2010, for the third year in a row" (Cisco, 3). That figure may not come as much of a surprise to many people. What is surprising, however, is that the use of mobile services overseas in areas beyond the power grid – meaning that there are parts of the world where households have cell phones but no electricity. As the Cisco study states:

> There are already 32 countries where mobile data has broken the electricity barrier. By the end of 2011, this effect will be visible at the regional level, when the total number of mobile users in Sub-Saharan Africa and Southeast Asia exceeds the total on-grid population in those regions. By the end of 2013, the number of mobile users in the Middle East will exceed the Middle Eastern on-grid population, and by 2015 the number of mobile users in South Asia (India and surrounding countries) will exceed the South Asian on-grid population (15).

On the surface, it may appear from the above statistics that for many people the need to communicate takes precedence over the need for basic electricity. It may seem that Maslow's hierarchy of needs, where basic physiological needs like shelter, have somehow gone out of whack and put cell phones at the top of the list. But that is not the case. For rural areas of Africa, mobile phones are simply the cheapest form of communication available. In the mid-1990s, African nations began to privatize their telephone monopolies. Competition among carriers meant they were selling "air time" in smaller and less expensive bundles. On a continent where there is "just one land line for every 33 people" and "only about 60 percent of Africans are within reach of a signal, the lowest level of penetration in the world, the technology is for many a social and economic godsend" (Lafraniere, 1). Charging phones with car batteries and by whatever means available, cell phones are helping people scrape out a living. As reported in *The New York Times*, an illiterate woman living on the Congo River tells customers to call her cell phone if they want to buy fish. Unable to put fish in a freezer, she keeps her fish in the river "tethered live on a string, until a call comes in" (Lafraniere, 1). Then she retrieves them and readies them for sale. The difference between poor rural women in Africa and us, at least for right now, is that they are not streaming video, 'Facebooking' their ex-girlfriend, or checking into FourSquare®, they are, as Robert Vamosi writes, "paying bills and seeking medical assistance when needed" (168). For many villagers in Africa, mobile phones are tools for realizing the most basic needs on Maslow's hierarchy. While certainly very basic by our standards, their mobile phones are what I would consider a necessity.

Mobile phones are a necessity for Americans as well. But like most things, we tend to abuse them. Food, water, sleep are obvious items required for human survival. But for some reason, many of us place communicating on our mobile phones above basic survival needs. If there is one thing that really annoys me in this word, it is people who talk on their cell phone while driving. I see people driving and talking on their cell phones constantly. I have seen all types of people chatting away on their phones – mostly oblivious to their surroundings. Where I live in North Carolina, there is a ban on cell phone use (handheld and hands-free) for bus drivers, "novice drivers" (95% of the driving public in my opinion, but not specifically defined by the DMV) and all drivers under the age of 18. There is also a ban on texting for all drivers. So while not illegal for most drivers, I would argue that one essentially has to "text" to make a call while driving. You need to take your eyes off the road to scroll through your contacts, find the person you wish to call and call them. An accident can happen in the time it takes to find a contact and make a call while driving.

It has gotten so bad that I decided to do an experiment and count the number of people I passed on my commute to work who were either texting or talking on their cell phone. I should point out that I have been criticized by some who claim that the very act of me counting people while driving is just as distracting as talking on a cell phone, so there is a level of hypocrisy in the nature of my study. I defend my research methods by pointing out that part of defensive driving is being aware of your surroundings and making eye contact with fellow drivers, as described by the Young Drivers ® program of Canada. I stand by my research methods and feel they are safe (for the most part).

My commute to work takes 25 minutes when traffic is clear. On part of the drive, Highway 40 opens up to 4 lanes. This stretch is a perfect spot for my experiment because it is almost exactly 10 miles long. For my experiment, I tried to keep certain constants. I drove at a consistent speed, always allowing traffic to pass me. I drove during the same time of day (5:30 p.m.) and in the same west-bound direction. I obviously did not count cars on the other side of the median as that is close to impossible. I just counted cars in my general vicinity, i.e., those who posed a direct threat to my personal safety. Below is the total number of people I either saw talking on their phone or texting (the people who were texting may also have been scrolling through their contacts about to make a call):

Monday – 13 (0 Texts)
Tuesday – 12 (0 Text)
Wednesday – 18 (3 Text)
Thursday – 18 (5 Text)
Friday – 15 (3 Text)
TOTAL = 76
TOTAL TEXT = 11
TOTAL MILES = 50

For a week in late April 2011, driving between Raleigh and Durham North Carolina, 1.52 people were seen talking on their cell phones for every mile driven during the midst of the 5:00pm rush hour. 0.22 people were seen texting and/or holding their phones searching for a contact. At one point within this study, I noticed five cars in a row where the driver was talking on his/her cell phone.

If global mobile data traffic continues to triple each year, and if state laws in North Carolina don't change, it is fair to expect that more than 1.52 people per every mile driven will be talking on their cell phone. I can only assume that that number will continue to go up. In an age of annoyance, we cannot underestimate the importance people place on speed and convenience over more basic things like personal safety.

The age of annoyance – minor injustices

We are the Dead. Short days ago
We lived, felt dawn, saw sunset glow,
Loved and were loved, and now we lie,
In Flanders fields.
– Lieutenant Colonel John McCrae

I am actually not that concerned about the threat talking while driving poses to my personal safety. What truly annoys me about people who talk on their cell phones while driving is that I find it to be a minor injustice; talking on a cell phone while driving violates my moral compass. University of Louisville psychologist Michael Cunningham considers such annoyances "norm violations." They are "intentional behaviors that are not directed at you personally but violate some standard that you have" (Lichtman, 147). I consider myself a very conscientious driver. I only stick to the left lane when passing. I always scan intersections before driving through them. I use my turn signals religiously. In short, I pay attention to myself and others while driving. As a result, I cannot stand people who do not reciprocate. You can always tell when someone answers a call while driving because they almost instantly slow down, even if they are in the passing lane. It takes them a moment to realize that they have lost momentum. Chances are they may check their blind spot but they almost never use their signal before slowly getting over so people can pass them. I find this inconsiderate. I know that people usually feel an urgent need to answer a call or send a text immediately, but there are rarely ever actual emergency calls that cannot wait until you reach your destination. What follows is sort of a web 2.0 take on an old cliché saying, but I am going to use it anyways – when I see someone chatting on their phone while driving, I want to say to them "listen, there is a young boy right now somewhere in Africa who has to walk 10 miles to find a lady with a car battery to charge his flip-phone to make a single call so he can buy some fish from a river, the least you can do is wait 10 minutes to reach your destination to make your call that's so damn important."

This nagging behavior makes me feel old, and I have no one to blame but myself for letting such annoyances get under my skin. Such annoyances, Flora Lichtman and Joe Palca write, represent the largest category of annoyances, i.e., those that "violate certain social rules or conflict with our value system or destroy a reasonable expectation" (134). I expect people to drive as well, if not better, than me and it annoys me when they don't. It is subjective as to whether this expectation is reasonable or not – given the population size and diversity found in the United States. Having driven in places like Germany and Japan where there are very high standards placed on drivers, I simply expect the same from the United States. Call me crazy; I just do. Perhaps the societal norm that states one should be a conscientious and good driver is not as pronounced here as it is in other areas of the world.

From a marketing and communication standpoint, I would like to share an interesting example of how norm violations can vary drastically between different countries. Remembrance Day and Veterans Day, on the surface, may appear to be similar holidays as they both take place on the same day, November 11. But in my experience, they are observed very differently.
Remembrance Day takes place in commonwealth countries. Like Veterans Day, it is a holiday that started after the end of the First World War to honor the men and women who died serving in combat. When I was growing up in Canada, Remembrance Day was always a very somber day. People wore Poppies above their hearts, the symbol of wartime remembrance. At school, we would normally have an assembly where everyone would observe a moment of silence and the Principle would give a presentation about Canada's involvement in times of war. Canadians are very patriotic so we would also discuss the importance of Lieutenant Colonel John McCrae, who wrote the poem *In Flanders Fields* that helped to immortalize the poppy as a symbol of remembrance, as corn poppies bloomed in between the trench lines on the Western front of WWI. News anchors, actors and celebrities in the weeks leading up to Remembrance Day can be seen wearing Poppies. The same is true in the UK. When "Harry Potter and the Deathly Hallows" had its London premiere on

November 11, 2010 in London, the film's stars were all seen wearing Poppies. While the gesture is normal to a UK audience, the US news media had to actually explain the significance. Yahoo News ran the headline "Seeing Red: Why the 'Harry Potter' Stars Wore Red Flowers on the Red Carpet" (Zap, 1). Celebuzz.com reported "Americans may have been befuddled by the red pins worn by Emma Watson, Daniel Radcliffe and the rest of *The Harry Potter and the Deathly Hallows* cast" (celebuzz.com).

I do not remember there ever being Remembrance Day sales in Canada. The holiday is not associated with shopping, a lesson that Eddie Bauer learned the hard way. In November 2010, an article by Michelle McQuigge posted on Global TV Edmonton's website states that "Eddie Bauer's week-long 'Remembrance Day' sale, launched in stores across Canada on Friday, sparked protests from veterans who felt disrespected by the American clothing giant" (McQuigge, 1). Both veterans and citizens voiced their disapproval on social network sites, calling the campaign insensitive. The article points out that Eddie Bauer President Neil Fisk issued a statement saying that the Canadian sale was based on a similar promotion held at its U.S. locations. "We appreciate the sensitivity around this holiday and the feedback we have received," Fisk writes, "we have tremendous respect for veterans across Canada and the U.S. and will adjust our marketing and communications accordingly" (McQuigge, 1). In response to the statement, the Director of Communications for The Royal Canadian Legion, Bob Butt, writes that his organization "does not like the fact that he's [Fisk] using Remembrance Day as a sales pitch" (McQuigge, 1).

Americans are also very patriotic, and it goes without saying that they honor veterans a great deal. Such brave men and women sacrifice greatly for their country and need to be recognized. I find it interesting, however, that Veterans Day in the US is celebrated much differently than Remembrance Day is in Canada and the UK. Veterans Day sales are an accepted norm in the US. You are expected to shop and people expect there to be sales. I know of a company that did a Veterans Day sale in the US entitled "Salute to Savings." The campaign brought in enough revenue to make it the best sales day of 2010 up to that point. The corresponding email message had an unsubscribe rate of less than 0.02%, a reasonable rate for most large-scale email marketing campaigns. Of that campaign, there was only one negative reply from a Briton who happened to have his billing address within the UK but his contact information set to the United States. The user's reply is as follows:

Date: 2010-11-11 09:01 AM
Subject: RE: Veterans Day Sale - VERY POOR MARKETING TASTE

This offer is in very poor taste given the context of the day. Cashing in on Remembrance Day, making money off the back of the dead, doesn't reflect well on your brand. Very disappointing email to receive.

Whoever is handling your marketing, I would seriously consider a change.

Because of a database anomaly, there was only one Briton who received the message that should not have. To him, there is a cultural norm that you do not market during Remembrance Day. He was obviously very annoyed with the message because it violates a high moral standard that he has. But within the United States, the Veterans Day sale was a record revenue generator with very little, if any, negative fall-out. There is simply a different societal expectation. In America, we do not find Veterans Day sales inappropriate or annoying. It is, right or wrong, simply part of our social milieu.

Talking on cell phones while driving or marketing during Remembrance Day clearly violate the Canadian moral compass. Ontario, for instance, has stricter rules than North Carolina when it comes to using cell phones while driving. The Ontario Provincial Police (OPP) did a press release in July 2011 with the tag line "Phone in One Hand, Ticket in the Other," informing Canadians of a distracted driving sweep that brought more than

1,600 citations in one week with fines of $155 for using handheld cell phones while driving – texting or not (OPP). The OPP cited that the "Canadian Automobile Association (CAA) ranked the distracted driver as its number one concern on the roads in 2010" (OPP). OPP Commissioner, Chris Lewis states that:

> I am astounded and dismayed at the number of drivers I see talking or texting on cell phones over the course of my travels. These people have no regard for the safety of their passengers or the people travelling around them whose lives they can end in a split second (OPP).

Without question, there are plenty of people like me in the United States who are annoyed with people talking on their cell phones while driving. With enough road fatalities, rules in the United States, I am sure, will become harsher like they are in Canada. But as of now, it seems to be a matter of societal norms, i.e., when do enough people in the US get annoyed by the issue that there becomes enough pressure to enact legislative change?

The age of annoyance – the new norm

Annoyance is mild anger. – Psychologist James Gross

We no longer read the manual before powering on; we demand intuitive interfaces that appear up and running right away. – Robert Vamosi

In my opinion, what has contributed most to our current age of annoyance is the societal norm that technology should provide us with countless options but also be fast, smart, intuitive, and very easy to use. We expect technology to possess such traits. When a device does not act in a manner becoming of a good piece of machinery, we get frustrated with it. Annoying computers are like annoying people and we get frustrated with them when they don't act the way they are supposed to.

In a study published in the *Journal of Educational Multimedia and Hypermedia,* Richard Ferdig and Punya Mishra examined people's emotional responses to computers when they felt that the computer had cheated them. Their findings suggest "that humans can get betrayed, get wounded pride, and in turn, can act spitefully towards computers in much the same way they do to humans" (Ferdig and Mishra, 146). The study begins by highlighting research from peer institutions like Stanford University, the University of Florida and Michigan State University that indicates that people tend to act polite towards machines, read gender and personalities into machines, are flattered by machines, and treat machines as teammates. It is argued that humans project emotions on machines when machines are viewed as social actors. Computers are an extension of who we are; thus, we expect them to follow the same social norms that we do. Measuring this fact is actually rather straightforward. As Ferdig and Mishra write: "start with any social situation where there are norms and rules, and thus expectations. Replace one of the human actors with a computer actor and the results of the social rule will essentially stay the same" (146). It is easy to think of countless such situations where you may have experienced this phenomenon. Replace the person in the passenger seat of your car with your GPS; you expect your GPS to give you the correct directions just as you would the person who is navigating. When either the GPS or the navigator does not, you get frustrated. Replace the soda fountain clerk with a Coke machine; you expect it to give you your Coke when you give it money. When it doesn't, you get pissed. Replace a phone operator with a machine; you expect it to understand basic English. You get the picture.

We get frustrated with machines because we are able to view them as surrogate humans – stand-ins that, while not equal, are still worthy of both our praise and displeasure. Part of the reason why people treat computers as social actors, Ferdig and Mishra argue, "is that today's computers are more sophisticated and capable of performing more complex and diverse tasks than ever before" (144). We are substituting humans with machines for more of our daily tasks. In turn, this greatly increases the odds of us getting frustrated with machines on any given day. This reality leads me to believe that marketers, designers, and engineers need to be mindful of what I call the "e-spot." The e-spot is your technological boiling point. With human interactions, it takes a while to get to this stage. An annoying co-worker or someone coughing throughout a movie will take a while before their behavior gets under our skin. With our interactions with machines, however, we reach the e-spot very quickly, sometimes almost instantly.

"Feature fatigue" is an example of how product designers unwittingly stumble upon the e-spot. University of Maryland Professor Roland Rust coined the term feature fatigue, describing it as mental exhaustion and stress caused by products that come with a large number of features. Feature fatigue "is the inevitable consequence of feature creep, the tendency for designers and programmers to bundle every feature they can imagine into every single product" (Surowiecki, 1). In an article in *The New Yorker*, writer James Surowiecki uses the example of cars to describe feature fatigue, stating:

> A product with too many features is likely to annoy consumers and generate bad word of mouth, as BMW's original iDrive system did. Intended to give drivers unprecedented control over navigation, temperature, and entertainment through a single device, it was so hard to use that it has been described as 'arguably the biggest corporate disaster' since New Coke.

I can imagine someone taking a BMW for a test drive and having a salesperson describe all of the features. As he cruised along the highway, the salesperson would activate the iDrive system for him, and the driver would be amazed by all the clever things it can do. Once he got the car home and no longer had the salesperson to coach him through it, his perception of the iDrive changes. As Surowiecki writes, "buyers want bells and whistles but users want something clear and simple" (1). In the case of cars, buyers and users have different e-spots. That is because buyers are able to deal with humans (salespeople) while users are forced to deal with machines (iDrive systems). Replace a human actor with a computer actor, and we will project our frustrations on the machine much faster than we will on a human.

Feature fatigue in BMWs shares similarities to what is known as the information-load paradigm, a concept that has been around for some time. The study of information overload began in 1975 with a paper by Jacoby, Speller and Berning. The study was concerned with the public policy of whether, when, and how consumers become overloaded with product information. Studies in information overload argue that:

> ... as a sort of 'information processing system,' human ability is subject to the same constraints as any sort of machine system; the human system is certainly limited in its capacity to do work, and, like any machine, exhibits problems of reliability as that capacity limitation is approached (Owen, 1).

Information overload deals with choice errors made by humans under conditions where there are countless selections. Overload occurs when a buyer cannot complete a purchase successfully. "An objectively inferior product choice is made by a high proportion of consumers under high load conditions," otherwise known as overload (Owen, 1). In an article entitled "Choose, Choose, Choose, Choose, Choose, Choose, Choose: Emerging and Prospective Research on the Deleterious Effects of Living in Consumer Hyperchoice" published in the *Journal of Business Ethics*, Mick et al report that information overload "relates to feelings of exasperation and grumpiness" for many people and can lead to "negative behavioral outcomes such as judgmentalism, impatience, and rudeness" (210). Like BMW's original iDrive, we may think that we want choice, but when it comes down to it, hyperchoice may simply lead to annoyance and frustration.

Such scenarios seem far too commonplace nowadays. It has become the new norm. We want fast and smart technology that can do a million things, but we want it to be easy and intuitive at the same time. We expect designers and industry professionals to develop technology with our unique dispositions in mind that anticipate our thresholds for annoyance – thresholds that are greatly diminished when a machine is used to replace a task normally done by a human. If our expectations are not met, we feel justified in voicing our anger and disapproval, provided the machine does not return a disapproving stare. Finally, all of these annoyances are exasperated by good old fashioned information overload, something that forces us to make bad decisions and can ignite spouts of rage. So how do we address this new norm? How do we function in an age of annoyance?

Digital detox

His mind moves forth only when some external thing has roused it. – Chuang Tzu

During my undergraduate studies, one of my favorite courses was Taoist Philosophy offered through the department of East Asian Studies at the University of Toronto. Prior to joining the class, I was warned that it filled up very quickly as students around campus praised both the Professor and subject matter for being intellectually stimulating without being a great deal of work. In the class, students were given the opportunity to write entire research papers based on a single word. The course also had very loose deadlines, i.e., whenever you felt like the paper was done (provided you got it to the Professor before the semester was over). Such laidback structure undoubtedly appealed to the minds of young and impressionable kids, but I like to think that it offered a refreshing break from the otherwise fast-paced and rigorous college life.

The structure of the course mirrored many aspects of Taoist Philosophy and in particular the ideas expressed in the *Chuang Tzu*, a 33 chapter book written sometime in the 4th century BCE. It is very difficult to describe Taoist Philosophy and the *Chuang Tzu*, as any efforts to do so, some would argue, are doomed to fail. Taoism can be experienced through simple spontaneous actions or cultivated over years of dedication and focus. Burton Watson, who has translated the *Chuang Tzu*, writes that many Chinese philosophers during the 4th century aimed to address the question of "how is man to live in a world dominated by chaos, suffering, and absurdity?" (3). Watson argues that Taoism's goal is to emancipate oneself from the struggles of everyday life, freeing us from the politics of "this and that." It is a sort of mystical "don't sweat the small stuff" approach to life.

In section 23 of the *Chuang Tzu*, the author(s) tell the story of a man named Nan-jung Chu. In a scene straight out of a Kung-Fu film, Chu travels deep into the mountains to visit an old Taoist sage Lao Tzu to seek guidance and answers to some of his worldly problems. When Chu arrives, Lao Tzu asks, "why did you come with all this crowd of people?" (Watson, 251). Chu looks around and sees no one else. The reader is meant to infer that "the crowd of people" represents all the excess baggage of ideas, beliefs, prejudices, misconceptions, and assumptions that Chu brought with him. Chu's only hope to finding the answers to his problems is to leave all his mental baggage at the door. In short, a higher understanding cannot be found without first clearing one's mind. This story has since been retold countless times in our popular culture narratives. From Luke Skywalker and Yoda in *Star Wars*, to Po and Shifu in *Kung Fu Panda*, to Beatrix Kiddo and Pai Mei in *Kill Bill Vol. 2*, modern day Nan-jung Chus continue to seek mental clarity by losing the crowd of "people" that follow them wherever they go.

Today, we carry greater mental baggage than ever before, only now it is in digital form. Rarely do we ever grant ourselves an idle moment of contemplation when we have constant access to the Internet in our pockets. Sitting on a park bench, riding the bus to work, walking – all moments that were once reserved for reflection are easily filled with emails, text and streaming video. In his book *The Shallows: What The Internet Is Doing To Our Brains*, Nicholas Carr argues that "calm, focused, undistracted, the linear mind is being pushed aside by a new kind of mind" (10). This new kind of mind, in my opinion, is a complete scatter brain. Our minds are in a million places at once and not focused on the present. Carr does point out the irony in that he claims that the Internet makes us scatter brains while he managed to focus his attention long enough to write a book. To complete his book, however, Carr moved from "a highly connected Boston" to the mountains of Colorado (198). He cancelled his Twitter account and put his Facebook profile on hold and most importantly he cut back on email. At first, he writes, "my synapses howled for their Net fix" (199). Like a junky or a gambling addict at a slot machine, his body craved those brief endorphin releases provided by status updates and image tags. But after his self-imposed digital detox, Carr states that "I started to feel generally calmer and more in control of my thoughts – less like a lab rat pressing a lever and more like, well, a human being. My brain could breathe again" (199). One could say that it was after he left his digital baggage at the door that Carr was able to see clearly again.

Carr's story somewhat echoes that of Matthew B. Crawford who wrote *The New York Times* bestseller *Shop Class as Soulcraft: an Inquiry into the Value of Work.* In his book, Crawford questions the pretensions of white-collared "knowledge work" and argues that manual labor can be more intellectually demanding and emotionally satisfying than that of seemingly more prestigious desk jobs. After completing a doctorate in political philosophy at the University of Chicago, Crawford took a job as an executive director of a Washington-based think tank. While he admits that the pay was good, Crawford states that his "sense of uselessness was dispiriting" (5). At the think tank, Crawford never saw any real output of his labor at the end of each day, and after five months, he quit to open a motorcycle repair shop. Crawford argues that we seem to have lost our "ethics of maintenance and repair" while many of us still strive "for some measure of self-reliance – the kind that requires focused engagement with our material things" (6-7). Whether it is repairing a motorcycle, tending to a garden, or simply fixing a leaky faucet, we do not seem to place as great an emphasis on self-reliance as we used to.

As someone who earns a living working with and on the Internet, both Crawford's and Carr's stories resonated with me. I do get the sense that my brain is constantly scattered on multiple tasks unable to focus completely on one thing. While I enjoy writing code and am emotionally fulfilled by the task, I do not get the same sense of accomplishment as I do after spending an entire afternoon doing yard work. I don't think that I am alone here. I have to assume that many of my peers involved in "knowledge work" who sit in front of the Internet all day have similar feelings.

My assumption seems validated when I see digital detox packages marketed to over-worked multi-tasking professionals. *The Wall Street Journal* reports that hotels have begun to offer discounts to guests that surrender their cell phones and computers at check in (Tergesen, 1). This clever promotion literally amounts to checking all your digital baggage at the door before getting an exfoliating mud bath.

Wandering deep into the mountains to seek the wisdom of a Taoist Sage, taking an extended digital detox in the mountains of Colorado to complete a book, and quitting one's job to open a motorcycle repair shop are all valiant pursuits, but they are not very practical for people with mortgages and bills to pay. In fact, I even question if Taoism in general is a practical philosophical approach to modern life. Sure, there are days when technology pisses me off so much that I just want to shave my head and join a commune, but such pipe dreams are just not practical. So while I have nothing but respect for Carr, Crawford and the sage wisdom of the ancient Chinese, I am stuck trying to find a way to address the age of annoyance while still earning a living working with technology. A digital detox, while a luxury like a vacation or spa day, is a nice idea and equally clever marketing trick; but, unfortunately, it is not a long-term solution to a growing issue.

OOO in the age of annoyance

One of the effects of living with electric information is that we live habitually in a state of information overload. There's always more than you can cope with. - Marshall McLuhan

In 2010, British graphic designer Rian Hughes published *CULT-URE,* a 364 page book packaged as a Gideon Bible, that examines "the changing nature of communication, perception and identity" (cult-ure.net). The book is a unique melding of graphics and images that raises questions about our modern media age, language, signs and symbols and is described as "your incisive survival guide for navigating the modern landscape of ideas" (cult-ure.net). Hughes covers a broad spectrum of topics with a section entitled "a surfeit of content" that pertains to our current age of information overload. He writes, "we are all becoming information managers, deciding what we can and cannot afford to ignore" (70). Some of us choose to ignore as little information as possible. We "tweet horizontally" as Scott Stratten calls it, where we fall asleep with our devices in hand and get up to check them first thing in the morning – constantly looking for and dealing with information updates. In such an environment, what constitutes a rare commodity? According to Hughes, the rarest commodity in the surfeit of content is your time (70). Our attention is an incredibly valuable resource. Our moms, friends, co-workers, RSS feeds, email subscriptions, Google alerts, and tweets are all bidding for our attention. Who gets it is ultimately up to each individual.

We have evolved over centuries to be able to selectively concentrate on certain aspects of our surroundings while ignoring other outside influences. We have that capability; it is simply a question of how and where we choose to exercise it online. In an article for *Publishers Weekly,* Duke University Professor Cathy N. Davidson describes "attention blindness [as] a basic feature of the brain – we pay attention to what's important at the moment by training ourselves to be oblivious to what's extraneous" (Boisvert, 1). Davidson refers to the "Invisible gorilla test," conducted by Daniel Simons of the University of Illinois at Urbana-Champaign and Christopher Chabris of Harvard University, which can be viewed at theinvisiblegorilla.com. The experiment involves watching a video of six uncoordinated research assistants awkwardly dribbling and passing basketballs. As you watch the video, you are asked to count how many times the players wearing white pass the balls. Three of the "players" wear white t-shirts while three wear black. Halfway through, a person in a black gorilla suit walks through the chaotic spectacle, pounds his chest, and leaves the frame. Most subjects apparently do not see the gorilla because they are concentrating on counting the passes. I'll admit, as a basketball fan, I was stuck trying to count the number of double dribbles, carries and walks each of these nonathletic research assistants could make in 30 seconds, but that's just me. Either way, the video helps highlight how human attention works. As Davidson points out in her new book, *Now You See It,* "the more you concentrate, the more other things you miss" (4). At times, while our attention is focused on one item, we can become essentially blind to other things within plain sight.

I have no idea what the future holds, but I am pretty sure that it will involve a lot more information. There will reach a point where our ability to be good information managers will determine whether this will remain an age of annoyance or become an age of great creative growth. Our ability to ignore gorillas that walk across our screens may turn out to be as much of an advantage as it is a disadvantage in the world of online distractions. Within the over-crowded media landscape there is a great deal of insight provided by real experts that we could easily overlook if and when we isolate ourselves in our respective corners of the Internet.

As a marketer, I originally set out to write a book to help marketing professionals find solutions to the communication challenges in an age of annoyance. Instead of offering advice, the book has turned out to be more a collection of observations that one can use to draw his or her own conclusions. What I have discovered is that information management has always been part of who we are as humans. We ignore some things while focusing on others. The digital world just puts a lot more stimuli in front of us in a short period of time. In response to this, we need to continue to refine and adjust our skills as information managers. Information management, like annoyance, is a relative and subjective phenomenon. We each have different e-spots – thresholds for annoyance. Information management solutions that work for me may fail miserably for someone else. Therefore, I really cannot offer any solutions that will work for the majority of the population – except one.

As someone who has worked in technology and digital marketing for a number of years now, I think that one of the best tools for good information management is a sincere Out of Office reply. In an era of insane information overload, the OOO acts as our individual declaration to the world that we are active information managers. Like the Pope's email message I received years ago, a good OOO lets the world know that you are choosing to focus your attention elsewhere. When I receive an OOO, I tend to feel empathy as opposed to annoyance with the individual. Even if the person's absence prevents me from accomplishing a task in the time frame I initially hoped for, I cannot fault the person. As discussed earlier, within a social interaction, replacing a human with a machine can lead to annoyance. One would expect automated messages like OOOs to be extremely frustrating as a result. However, if written with a level of sincerity, an OOO can instill that very human emotion – empathy.

Duke Professor and best-selling author Dan Ariely is an information manager of the highest order. Between his blog, speaking engagements, books and Twitter feed, he has to be one of the busiest academics anywhere. Alone, there is no way he could effectively answer all of the emails he must get in a given day. He has managed to construct a wonderfully sincere and highly informative OOO. He writes:

>*Dear Friend,*
>
>*Thanks for your email.*

Chances are that you won't hear back from me. But please don't take it personally. It's just that my hands don't work very well, and typing causes a great amount of pain. To complicate matters, the overwhelming amount of email I get makes it impossible for me to keep up.

So for now I am going to read email but not respond to most of it. I'm not crazy about this approach but it's the best approach I have right now.

I also created a "frequently asked questions" section here:

http://www.danariely.com/faq

Ariely's FAQs link leads to a series of short web videos where he answers questions many people have for him. This OOO is an elegant solution to an otherwise annoying problem – email overload. The approach also offers, through the use of video, a more personalized and rich experience than your typical OOO: "thanks for your message, I will reply soon."

So when it comes time for you to go on your next digital detox, don't just write a boring OOO. Make it clever. I have even included some of the more interesting OOO replies I have collected over the years for inspiration. These OOOs also offer a nice contrast to the angry unsubscribes listed within the introduction of this book.

In the age of annoyance, it is not just technology that is annoying: we are annoying as well. So the least we can do is try to let folks know that their messages are important to us ... just not right now.

.... so I'm at home cooking for the party tonight! And annoying my family!

I promise I'll get back to you after the weekend

(hey - 40's not such a bad number is it?)
....

Left the sanity of the Swiss vineyards for the highlands and heathens of Scotland for a week of sipping malts, and roaming in the gloaming, with a Bonnie near the Clyde. I used to have a lap-top as I did a lap, but both have been purloined from my loins by a damn Yankee so no communications for a week. If urgent, and I really mean so urgent it is a matter of strife and breath send a short text to.
....

I am currently taking a much anticipated holiday in the northern hemisphere and will return to work on Monday 11th October.

As I am a workaholic I will be checking my emails frequently and voice messages when I can sneak it.

If you require immediate help with anything, please contact...
....

off to Kalamazoo
yes it's true...
be back before the Moon is Full
....

Dear All

I will be out of the office all day on Monday Feb 28. I will also be our of [sic] the office on the MORNING OF MY BIRTHDAY, Tuesday MARCH 1st as I will be crying that I am now old. Flowers and gifts of sympathy are fine by me ☺

I will return all calls and emails later on Tues 1st.
....

Thank you for attempting to contact me. I am quite likely stuck under
something heavy as I am taking some time off to move from one house to
another. I will attempt to catch up with my emails and phone messages after
the 1st of July.

Thank you for your patience as I disorder and reorder my life's possessions.
....

Hi there, this is me.

I am currently not present at the mothership. Actually I'm practicing the art of human hibernation. Scientists believe that once we master this skill, it will be humanly possible to visit other galaxies. I'm not sure whether I'd like to be part of such an expedition. I'm probably too tall anyway. And I love my French cheese. French cheese doesn't do well in space they say. Anyway, I do like the thought of saving up energy, by lowering my body temperature and heartbeat. Oh and there's the added bonus of living of [sic] my stored body fats. I will get back to you once I awake. That'll be October 18th, 2010.

....

Hello,

I'm in the middle of nowhere, doing nothing much of anything until the end of October.

Once I'm back in the land of technology I'll contact you.

Be well,
....

Hi,

I'm on a strict email diet - less email, more productivity - so I am only checking email a few times each day. But I do want to hear from you. If you need my attention immediately, you can reach me here:
....

hi & thanks for your email.

It's too beautiful outside today - needed to take the afternoon off!
If this is urgent, please text or call my cell -

I"ll be back tomorrow

cheers
....

I will be away for a fortnight. I hope to be back at my desk on August 1th. Try to go on without me. I know you can and I'll be very grateful for that.

Regards.

....

I am on the beach in mauii hawaiiiiiii.....i cant read your email cos im busy workin on my tan...see ya when i get back home...dont be jelous...pass me another mai tai....go away now...im busy

....

Off the planet

Major Tom to Ground Control...

Here am I sitting in my tin can, far above the Moon...

Actually I'm orbiting planet France for the month of September. I'll still get to email but if there's something of a delay, I trust you'll understand.

Thanks

....

Bibliography:

Abella, Irving. & Troper, Harold,. (1983). *None Is Too Many: Canada and the Jews of Europe 1933-1948.* Lester Publishing Limited. Toronto.

Aboujaoude, Elias. (2011). *Vitrually You: The Dangerous Powers of the E-Personality.* W.W. Norton & Company,Inc. New York, NY.

Adams, Debra. (2006). "Journalism, citizens and blogging." In *Proceedings Communications Policy and Research Forum.* University of Technology Sydney (UTS) Australia.

Anderson, Chris. (2006). *The Long Tail: Why the Future of Business Is Selling Less of More.* Hyperion. New York, NY.

Bailey, Brian., Carlis, John V., & Konstan, Josheph A. (2001). "The Effects of Interruptions on Task Performance, Annoyance, and Anxiety in the User Interface." University of Minnesota Department of Computer Science and Engineering Minneapolis, MN 55455.

Bala, Nicholas. (2002). *Youth Criminal Justice Law.* Irwin Law. Pp. 381-388. Toronto.

Beham, Günter,. Costa, Cristina,. Ebner, Martin,. & Reinhardt, Wolfgang,. (2009). "How People are using Twitter during Conferences" In Creativity *and Innovation Competencies on the Web.* Hornung-Prähauser, V., Luckmann, M. (Ed.) Proceeding of 5. EduMedia conference, p. 145-156, Salzburg.

Bilton, Nick. (2009). "The American Diet: 34 Gigabytes a Day" In *The New York Times.* December 9, 2009, 7:00 AM http://bits.blogs.nytimes.com/2009/12/09/the-american-diet-34-gigabytes-a-day/

Boisvert, Will. (2011). "Seeing the Gorilla in the Room: PW Talks with Cathy N. Davidson" In *Publishers Weekly*. July 01, 201i.
http://www.publishersweekly.com/pw/by-topic/authors/interviews/article/47854-seeing-the-gorilla-in-the-room-pw-talks-with-cathy-n-davidson.html

Boutin, Paul. (2007). "The iPhone Menace: Only the BlackBerry can save our nation's productivity." In *Slate Magazine*.
http://www.slate.com/id/2173481/fr/flyout

Bradley, Curtis,. Cole, David,. Dellinger, Walter,. Dworkin, Ronald,. Epstein, Richard,. Heymann, Philip B., et al., (2006). "On NSA Spying: A Letter to Congress" In *The New York Review of Books* - Volume 53, Number 2.
http://www.nybooks.com/articles/18650

Brogan, Chris,. & Smith, Julien. (2010). *Trust Agents: Using the Web to Build Influence, Improved Reputation, and Earn Trust*. John Wiley & Sons, Inc. New Jersey.

Buiani, Roberta. (2009). "Viral Games in the Networked World" In *The Spam Book: On Viruses, Porn, And Other Anomalies From The Dark Side Of Digital Culture*. Parikka, Jussi,. & Sampson, Tony D,. (eds). Hampton Press, Inc. New Jersey.

Carr, Nicholas. (2010). *The Shallows: What The Internet Is Doing To Our Brains*. W.W. Norton & Company,Inc. New York, NY.

Carton, Bruce. (2009). "Twittering From the Courtroom? Not So Fast" In *Legalblogwatch.typepad.com*. November 9, 2009.
http://legalblogwatch.typepad.com/legal_blog_watch/2009/11/twitter-from-the-courtroom-not-in-the-middle-district-of-georgia.html

celebuzz.com., (2010). "What's Up With Those Red 'Harry Potter' Poppy Pins?" November 12, 2010.

Cohen, Adam. (2010). "Should Twitter Have a Seat in Court?" In *Time Magazine*. Wednesday, Dec. 22, 2010.
http://www.time.com/time/nation/article/0,8599,2039400,00.html

Colopy, Joe. (2011). "Email Service Providers are the New Banks" In *joeism.com*. April 04, 2011.
http://joeism.com/2011/04/04/email-service-providers-are-the-new-banks/

Crawford, Matthew B. (2009). *Shop Class as Soulcraft: An Inquiry into the Value of Work*. Penguin Books. New York, NY.

Cervantes, Adriana. (2010). "Will Twitter Be Following You in the Courtroom?: Why Reporters Should Be Allowed to Broadcast During Courtroom Proceedings" In *Hastings Communication & Entertainment Law Journal*, Vol. 33, p. 133, 2010

Cisco Systems Inc. (2011). "Cisco Visual Networking Index: Global Mobile Data Traffic Forecast Update, 2010–2011." Printed in USA
http://www.cisco.com/en/US/solutions/collateral/ns341/ns525/ns537/ns705/ns827/white_paper_c11-520862.html

Davidson, Cathy N. (2011). *Now You See It: How The Brain Science Of Attention Will Transform The Way We Live, Work, And Learn.* Viking. New York, NY.

Decker, Stefan,. Hausenblas, Michael,. Kärger, Philipp,. Olmedilla, Daniel,. Passant, Alexandre, & Polleres, Axel,. (2008). "Enabling Trust and Privacy on the Social Web." W3C Workshop on the Future of Social Networking, 15-16 January 2009, Barcelona.

Deuze, Mark. (2004). "What is Multimedia Journalism?" In *Journalism Studies*, Volume 5, Number 2, 2004, pp. 139-152

Blaggs, Alex. (2011). "Bizwords" In *Fast Company*. Issue 155. May 2011. Mansueto Ventures, LLC. New York, NY. Pg. 37.

Doctorow, Cory. (2009). "Writing in the Age of Distraction." In *Locus Magazine*, January 2009.
http://www.locusmag.com/Features/2009/01/cory-doctorow-writing-in-age-of.html

Domingo, David., & Heinonen, Ari., (2008). "Weblogs and Journalism: A Typology to Explore the Blurring Boundaries" In *Nordicom Review* 29 (2008) 1.

Dvorak, John C. (2009). "9 Reasons E-Mail Is Dead" In *PC Magazine*. March 16, 2009.
http://www.pcmag.com/article2/0,2817,2343209,00.asp

Eggen, Dan. (2006) "White House Dismissed '02 Surveillance Proposal" In *Washington Post*. A SECTION. January 26, 2006.

Elgan, Mike. (2011). "Larry Page's first blunder" In *CompuerWorld*. April 9, 2011.
http://www.computerworld.com/s/article/9215666/Larry_Page_s_first_blunder?taxonomyId=169&pageNumber=1

Epsilon.com. (2011). "Epsilon Notifies Clients of Unauthorized Entry into Email System" April 1, 201.
http://www.epsilon.com/News%20&%20Events/Press%20Releases%202011/Epsilon_Notifies_Clients_of_Unauthorized_Entry_into_Email_System/p1057-13

Epsilon.com. (2011). "Epsilon Unveils Innovative Security Enhancements to Global Email Marketing Platform: Unique Custom Security Solution from Verizon Enables Advanced Intrusion Detection; Epsilon Introduces IP White Listing and Two-Factor Authentication" Dallas, Texas – June 29, 2011.
http://www.epsilon.com/apac/News%20&%20Events/Press-Releases-2011//p1121-l3

Fallows, James. (1997). *Breaking the News: How the Media Undermine American Democracy*. Random House, New York.

Ferdig, Richard E., & Mishra, Punya., (2004). "Emotional Responses to Computers: Experiences in Unfairness, Anger, and

Spite" In *Journal of Educational Multimedia and Hypermedia*, Vol. 13, 2004.
http://punya.educ.msu.edu/publications/journal_articles/Ferdig_Mishra_JEMH04.pdf

Forster, E. M. (1909). *The Machine Stops*. http://gutenberg.org

Freeman, John. (2009). *The Tyranny of E-Mail*. Simon & Schuster, Inc. New York, NY.

Gleick, James. (2011). *The Information: A History A Theory A Flood*. Pantheon Books, New York.

Globe Editorial. (2011). "Vancouver can now hold the mob to account" In *The Globe And Mail*. Jun. 21, 2011
http://www.theglobeandmail.com/news/opinions/editorials/vancouver-can-now-hold-the-mob-to-account/article2069813/

Godin, Seth. (1999). *Permission Marketing™: Turning Strangers into Friends, and Friends into Customers*. Simon & Schuster. New York, NY.

Godin, Seth. (2005). *All Marketers Are Liars: The Power of Telling Authentic Stories in a Low-Trust World*. Portfolio. New York, NY.

Godwin, Mike. (1994). "Meme, Counter-meme" In *Wired* Magazine. Issue 2.10. October 1994.
http://www.wired.com/wired/archive/2.10/godwin.if_pr.html

Greenwald, Glenn. (2006). "The New York Times' complicity in Bush's illegal eavesdropping" In *Unclaimed Territory*. December 17, 2006.
http://glenngreenwald.blogspot.com/2005_12_01_archive.html

Greenwald, Glenn. (2006). "The simplicity of the NSA scandal" In *Unclaimed Territory*. January 5, 2006.
http://glenngreenwald.blogspot.com/2006_01_01_archive.html

Greenwald, Glenn. (2006) "The Administration's new FISA defense is factually false." In *Unclaimed Territory*. January 24, 2006.
http://glenngreenwald.blogspot.com/2006_01_01_archive.html

Helprin, Mark. (2009). *Digital Barbarism: A Writer's Manifesto*. HarperCollins Publishing. New York, NY.

Hemming, Jon,. & Fincher, Christina,. (2009). "M16 chief's family life posted on Facebook" Reuters. London. Sun Jul 5, 2009 3:09pm BST
http://uk.reuters.com/article/2009/07/05/uk-britain-mi-idUKTRE56402R20090705

Homer-Dixon, Thomas. (2007). *The Upside of Down: Catastrophe, Creativity, and the Renewal of Civilization*. Vintage Canada. Toronto.

Hope, Alan. (2011). "Belgocide book causes international ire" In *Flanders Today*. June 21, 2011
http://www.flanderstoday.eu/content/offside-31

Hughes, Rian,. (2010). *CULT-URE*. ©Fiell Publishing Ltd. China.

The Independent. (2011) "Twitter index: live tweets of Osama Bin Laden's death" In *The Independent*. Monday, 2 May 2011
http://www.independent.co.uk/life-style/gadgets-and-tech/twitter-index-live-tweets-of-osama-bin-ladens-death-2277902.html

Jenkins, Holman W. Jr. (2010). "Google and the Search for the Future: The Web icon's CEO on the mobile computing revolution, the future of newspapers, and privacy in the digital age." In *The Wall Street Journal*. August 14, 2010.
http://online.wsj.com/article/SB10001424052748704901104575423294099527212.html

Keen, Andrew. (2007). *The Cult of the Amateur: How Blogs, MySpace, YouTube, and the Rest of Today's User-Generated*

Media Are Destroying Our Economy, Our Culture, and Our Values. Doubleday. New York, NY.

LaFraniere, Sharon. (2005) "Cellphones Catapult Rural Africa to 21st Century" in *The New York Times*. August, 25, 2005.

Lanier, Jaron. (2010). *You Are Not A Gadget: A Manifesto*. Alfred A. Knopf. New York, NY.

Leamer, Laurence. (2008). "Jewish Circuit's Faith is Shaken" In *The New York Post*. December 13, 2008.
http://www.nypost.com/p/news/item_onDxmPAYLnhLSwj7ZjD udN

Lears, Jackson. (1994). Fables *of Abundance: A Cultural History of Advertising in America*. BasicBooks. New York, N.Y.

Lichtman, Flora,. & Palca, Joe,. (2011). *Annoying: The Science of What Bugs Us*. John Wiley & Sons, Inc. Hoboken, New Jersey.

Lih, Andrew. (2004). "Wikipedia as Participatory Journalism: Reliable Sources?
Metrics for evaluating collaborative media as a news resource" In *5th International Symposium on Online Journalism* (April 16-17, 2004).

Lowrey, Wilson & Anderson, Williams., (2006). "The Journalist Behind the Curtain: Participatory Functions on the Internet and their Impact on Perceptions of the Work of Journalism" In *Journal of Computer-Mediated Communication* Volume 10, Issue3.

Madison, Lucy. (2011). "Glenn Beck criticized for comparing Norway victims to 'Hitler Youth'" in cbsnews.com. July 26, 2011 6:04 PM.
http://www.cbsnews.com/8301-503544_162-20083816-503544.html

Marshall, Edward. (2009). "Burglar leaves his Facebook page on victim's computer" In *The* Journal. September 16, 2009.
http://www.journal-news.net/page/content.detail/id/525232.html

Mailchimp. (2010). "Email Maketing Benchmarks by Industry" December 15, 2010.
http://mailchimp.com/resources/research/email-marketing-benchmarks-by-industry/

McLuhan, Marshall. (1967). *The Best of Ideas*. CBC Radio, 1967
http://faculty.uml.edu/sgallagher/marshall_mcluhan.htm

McQuigge, Michelle. (2010). "Eddie Bauer's 'Remembrance Day Sale' angers veterans" The Canadian Press: Monday, November 8, 2010.
http://www.globaltvedmonton.com/Eddie+Bauer+Remembrance+Sale+angers+veterans/3795568/story.html

Mick, David Glen,. Broniarczk, Susan M,. & Haidt, Jonathan,. (2004) "Choose, Choose, Choose, Choose, Choose, Choose, Choose: Emerging and Prospective Research on the Deleterious Effects of Living in Consumer Hyperchoice" In *Journal of Business Ethics*. 52: 207–211, 2004. 2004 Kluwer Academic Publishers. Printed in the Netherlands

Moschella, William E. (2005). "U. S. Department of Justice Letter." December 22, 2005. http://cryptome.org/doj-nsa-spy.htm

Mulpuru, Sucharita. (2011). "Keynote Address" At *Bronto Summit 2011*. Chapel Hill, NC.

Nip, Joyce. (2006). "Exploring the Second Phase of Public Journalism" In *Journalism Studies* Vol. 7, No 2, Routledge.

Oatney, David. (2005). "Holding the President to account" In *The World According to Oatney*. December 18, 2005.
http://oatneyworld.blogspot.com/2005_12_18_archive.html

Ontario Provincial Police. (2011). "OPP MEAN SERIOUS BUSINESS GOING INTO WEEK #2 OF DISTRACTED DRIVING CAMPAIGN." July 8 2011.
http://www.opp.ca/ecms/index.php?id=405&nid=636

Owen, Robert S. (1992). "Clarifying the Simple Assumption of the Information Load Paradigm" In Advances *in Consumer Research Volume 19*, eds. John F. Sherry, Jr. and Brian Sternthal, Provo, UT : Association for Consumer Research, Pages: 770-776. http://www.acrwebsite.org/volumes/display.asp?id=7387

Paasonen, Susanna. (2009). "Pornography Spam as Boundary Work" In *The Spam Book: On Viruses, Porn, And Other Anomalies From The Dark Side Of Digital Culture*. Parikka, Jussi and Sampson, Tony D,. (eds). Hampton Press, Inc. New Jersey.

Parr, Ben. (2011). "The Past, Present & Future of Email [INFOGRAPHIC]." In *Mashable*. May 6, 2011.
http://mashable.com/2011/05/05/past-present-future-email-infographic/

PEW Research. "Bloggers: A portrait of the internet's new storytellers"
http://www.pewinternet.org/report_display.asp?r=186

PEW Research. "Blogging is bringing new voices to the online world"
http://www.pewinternet.org/PPF/r/130/press_release.asp

Quain, John R. (2010). "Is E-Mailo Dead?" In *Fox News*. November 16, 2010.
http://www.foxnews.com/scitech/2010/11/16/is-email-dead-facebook-gmail-aol/

Rashid, Fahmida Y. (2011). "Congress Demanding Epsilon Release More Details About Data Breach" In *eWeek.com*. April 09, 2011.
http://www.eweek.com/c/a/Security/Congress-Demanding-Epsilon-Release-More-Details-About-Data-Breach-326688/

Rayport, Jeffrey. (1996). "The Virus of Marketing" In *Fast Company*. December 31, 1996.
http://www.fastcompany.com/magazine/06/virus.html

Reese, Stephen D., Rutigliano, Luo,. Hyun, Kideuk., & Jaekwan, Jeong., (2007). "Mapping the blogosphere: Professional and citizen-based media in the global news arena" In *Journalism*, Vol. 8, No. 3, 235-261DOI: 10.1177/1464884907076459.
http://jou.sagepub.com/cgi/reprint/8/3/235

Reese, Stephen. (2001). "Understanding the Global Journalist: a hierarchy-of-influences approach" In *Journalism Studies*, Vol2, Number 2, 2001.

Reynolds, Glenn. (2005). "DOMESTIC SPYING BY THE NSA?" December, 16, 2005.
http://pajamasmedia.com/instapundit/2005/12/page/3/

Risen, James,. & Lichtblau, Eric,. (2005). "Bush Lets U.S. Spy on Callers Without Courts" In *The New York Times.* December 16, 2005.
http://www.nytimes.com/2005/12/16/politics/16program.html?scp=22&sq=December%2016,%202005&st=cse

Risen, James,. & Lichtblau, Eric,. (2009). "Court Affirms Wiretapping Without Warrants" In *The New York Times.* January 15, 2009
http://www.nytimes.com/2009/01/16/washington/16fisa.html?_r=1&hp

Rothfuss, Patrick. (2007). *The Name of the Wind*. Daw Books, Inc. New York.

Rubin, Victoria., & Liddy, Elizabeth. (2006). "Assessing Credibility of Weblogs." *School for Information Studies*. Syracuse University.

Salter, Lee. (2006). "Democracy & Online News: Indymedia and the Limits of Participatory Media" In *Scan Journal* Vol 3. Number 1 June 2006.

Scanlon, Jessie. (2007). "Jeffrey Zeldman: King of Web Standards." In *Businessweek.com*. August, 6, 2007. http://www.businessweek.com/innovate/content/aug2007/id2007 086_670396.htm

Shaw, Gillian. (2011). "Twitter, Facebook collide with Canada's Elections Act." In *The Vancouver Sun*. April 21, 2011. http://www.vancouversun.com/news/Twitter+Facebook+collide+with+Canada+Elections/4658099/story.html

Spark, David. (2010). "I could just unsubscribe from your mailing list, but I'd rather be a jackass." On Spark Minute. http://www.sparkminute.com/ http://www.sparkminute.com/2010/09/23/i-could-just-unsubscribe-from-your-mailing-list-but-id-rather-be-a-jackass/

Steiner, Christopher. (2010). "Meet The Fastest Growing Company Ever." In *Forbes Magazine*. August 30, 2010. http://www.forbes.com/forbes/2010/0830/entrepreneurs-groupon-facebook-twitter-next-web-phenom.html

Stephenson, Neal. (1992). *Snow Crash*. Bantam Books. New York, NY.

Stratten, Scott. (2010). *Unmarketing: Stop Marketing. Start Engaging*. John Wiley & Sons, Inc. Hoboken, New Jersey.

Surowiecki, James. (2007). "Feature Presentation" In *The New Yorker*. May 28, 2007. http://www.newyorker.com/talk/financial/2007/05/28/070528ta_talk_surowiecki

Tapscott, Don., & Williams, Anthony D., (2006). *Wikinomics: How Mass Collaboration Changes Everything*. Penguin Group. Toronto, Ontario.

Tergesen, Anne. (2011). "When Guests Check In, Their iPhones Check Out." In *The Wall Street Journal*. JULY 5, 2011. http://online.wsj.com/article/SB10001424052702304584004576417942784252336.html

The Telegraph. (2011). "Swearing can help relieve pain, study claims." Sunday 14 May 2011. http://www.telegraph.co.uk/science/8458163/Swearing-can-help-relieve-pain-study-claims.html

Trippi, Joe. (2004). *The Revolution Will Not be Televised: Democracy, The Internet, and The Over Throw of Everything*. HarperCollins, New York, NY.

Tumber, Howard.. (2001). "Democracy In the Information Age: The Role of the Fourth Estate in Cyberspace" In *Information, Communication & Society*, 4:1. City University, London UK.

Tseng, H., Fogg, B.J. (1999). "Credibility and computing technology. Communications of the ACM." 42(5), 39-44.

Turkle, Sherry. (2011). *Alone Together: Why We Expect More From Technology And Less From Each Other*. Basic Books. New York, NY.

Vaidhyanathan, Siva. (2011). *The Googlization of Everything (AND WHY WE SHOULD WORRY)*. University of California Press, Berkely, Los Angeles.

Vascellaro, Jessica. (2009). "Why Email No Longer Rules ... And what that means for the way we communicate." In *The Wall Street Journal*. October 12, 2009. http://online.wsj.com/article/SB10001424052970203803904574431151489408372.html

Wasserman, Todd. (2011). "Why Your Email Inbox Is Bringing Home the Bacon [INFOGRAPHIC]" In *Mashable*. March 22, 2011.

http://mashable.com/2011/03/22/bacon-infographic/

Watson, Burton (trans). (1968). *The Complete Works of Chuang Tzu*. Columbia University Press. New York, NY.

White, Charlie. (2011). "Email Provider Epsilon Responsible For Gigantic Security Breach" In *Mashable*. April 3, 2011.

Vamosi, Robert. (2011). *When Gadgets Betray Us: The Dark Side of our Infatuation with New Technologies*. Basic Books. New York, NY.

Yardley, William. (2011). "A Fraud Played Out on Family and Friends." In *The New York Times*. May 26, 2011.
http://www.nytimes.com/2011/05/27/us/27ponzi.html

Zaller, John. (1999). *A Theory of Media Politics: How the Interest of Politicians, Journalists, and Citizens Shape the News*. University of Chicago Press. Chicago, Illinois.

Zap, Claudine. (2010). "Seeing Red: Why the 'Harry Potter' Stars Wore Red Flowers on the Red Carpet" Friday, November 12, 2010.
http://blog.movies.yahoo.com/blog/118-seeing-red-why-the-harry-potter-stars-wore-red-flowers-on-the-red-carpet?nc

Zax, David. (2011). "The Epsilon Breach: How Worried– and Angry– Should You Be?" In *Fast Company*. April 5, 2011.
http://www.fastcompany.com/1744738/the-epsilon-breach-should-you-be-angry-worried-or-bored

Zittrain, Jonathan. (2008). *The Future of the Internet And How to Stop It*. Yale University Press. London.

Audio files:

60 Minutes Overtime. (2011). "Obama on bin Laden: The full '60 Minutes' Interview." May 8, 2011 7:07 PM.
http://www.cbsnews.com/8301-504803_162-20060530-10391709.html?tag=cbsnewsMainColumnArea.1

"David Cameron on Absolute Radio." 13 March 2010.
http://www.absoluteradio.co.uk/onair/breakfast/blog/?id=122192&mode=post&s=1

Global News. (2011). "Nathan Kotylak: Rioter Apology FULL INTERVIEW." Monday, June 20, 2011 12:49 PM.
http://www.globalnews.ca/Nathan+Kotylak+Rioter+Apology+FULL+INTERVIEW/4975749/story.html

Global News. (2011). "Mob mentality persists in virtual riot." Saturday, June 25, 2011
http://www.globalnews.ca/mentality+persists+virtual+riot/5005366/story.html

McKinney Borind Tweets
http://mckinney.com/work/clients/mckinney/re-cycled-tweets

NMAWorldEdition. (2011). "Vancouver Riots 2011: Fans rage as Canucks lose Stanley Cup"
http://www.youtube.com/watch?&v=8LBxFmixh70

NOFX. (2003). "Idiots Are Taking Over" In "War On Errorism." Fat Wreck Chords.

Tweets:

Joe Newton
@TheJoeNewton Brooklyn
Designer, illustrator. And type geek for Veer
http://josephnewton.com/
http://shop.ilovetypography.com/product/google-before-you-tweet

Twitter by the numbers:
http://blog.twitter.com/2011/03/numbers.html

@zeldman
Jeffrey Zeldman
http://twitter.com/#!/zeldman/status/42674770592006144

Websites:

American Civil Liberties Union
http://www.aclu.org/safefree/nsaspying/34152prs20080219.html

Canadian Broadcast Corporation
http://www.cbc.radio-canada.ca/about/

Captain Vancouver
http://publicshamingeternus.wordpress.com/\

Facebook Justice
http://facebookjustice.wordpress.com/

Google Search Algorithm:
http://www.google.com/corporate/tech.html

Legal Guide for Bloggers
http://www.eff.org/issues/bloggers/legal

Media Bloggers Association
http://www.mediabloggers.org/
Momspam

http://www.momspam.net/

NSA blogger's compilation
http://www.theleftcoaster.com/archives/006455.php

Society of Professional Journalists
http://www.spj.org/

Society of Professional Journalists – Code of Ethics
http://www.spj.org/ethicscode.asp

Gavin Jocius has worked in digital marketing and electronic communications since the late 1990s. Having worked as the Director of Information Technology and Marketing Manager for both academic institutions and global organizations, he understands the many subtle and overt ways in which technology can both liberate and annoy. While at times a seemingly impossible task, Gavin aims to avoid annoying the two loves in his life – his wife Leann and his daughter Lyra. Gavin holds degrees from the University of Toronto, Sheridan College and Duke University.

www.ingramcontent.com/pod-product-compliance
Lightning Source LLC
Chambersburg PA
CBHW021959170526
45157CB00003B/1070